The Ultimate Book of Wedding Lists

 FROM 

WedSpace.com

Checklists, Options, Things to Consider, and Questions to Ask to help you plan the wedding of your dreams!

From America's Top Wedding Experts
Elizabeth & Alex Lluch
Authors of Over 3 Million Books Sold

WS Publishing Group
San Diego, California

The Ultimate Book of Wedding Lists
from WedSpace.com

By Elizabeth & Alex Lluch
America's Top Wedding Experts

Published by WS Publishing Group
San Diego, California 92119

Design by:
Sarah Jang, WS Publishing Group

Cover photo credit:
Karen French
Karen French Photography
(800) 734-6219
E-mail: info@karenfrenchphotography.com
Website: www.karenfrenchphotography.com
Available nationally and internationally
Based in Orange County, California

For Inquiries:
Log on to www.WSPublishingGroup.com
E-mail info@WSPublishingGroup.com

ISBN-13: 978-1-934386-83-5

Printed in China

Table of Contents

- ❊ Wedding Planning Timeline 7
- ❊ Wedding Budget 15
- ❊ Ceremony 29
- ❊ Attire 47
- ❊ Photography 75
- ❊ Videography 95
- ❊ Stationery 103
- ❊ Reception 135
- ❊ Music 171

INTRODUCTION

- Bakery 193
- Flowers 205
- Transportation 229
- Rental Items 237
- Gifts 251
- Parties 255
- Planning a Green Wedding 263
- Miscellaneous 273
- Do's & Don'ts 285
- Wedding Traditions 291
- Wedding Formations 295
- Wedding Party Responsibilities 301
- Who Pays For What 309
- Things to Bring 313
- Honeymoon 317
- Tell Us About Your Wedding 347

Introduction

Your wedding will be one of the happiest days of your life! Planning a wedding can be fun and exciting, but it can also be a bit overwhelming. Use this book to keep track of everything you need to do to have the wedding of your dreams!

About WedSpace.com

WedSpace.com is the fastest-growing online bridal community, designed for both engaged and married couples to connect with other brides, friends, family, wedding vendors and much more. WedSpace.com is an invaluable resource for planning a wedding, offering articles, news, polls, events, groups, media, and more.

WedSpace.com members can:

- Video chat live with guests and vendors
- Upload wedding music, photos, and videos
- Create blogs
- Post their wedding planning questions for experts and other brides to answer

WedSpace.com has created *The Ultimate Book of Wedding Lists from WedSpace.com* to help eliminate the stress of planning your wedding. This book contains hundreds of lists, checklists, timelines and comparison charts to keep you organized.

First, a comprehensive budget analysis outlines all the expenses incurred in a wedding. Next, you'll find Options, Things to Consider, Questions to Ask, Tips to Save Money, Unique Alternatives, and

INTRODUCTION

more for each aspect of the wedding. You'll also enjoy reading the Do's and Don'ts of planning and hosting your wedding, as well the significance of wedding traditions and a list of responsibilities for each member of your wedding party. We also provide traditional formations for the ceremony and receiving line for both Jewish and Christian weddings.

Lastly, we have included a section to help you prepare for your honeymoon. The worksheets and checklists in this chapter will help you choose your ideal destination and develop a budget and plan every detail of your dream vacation.

We are confident that this book will reduce the stress of planning a wedding and will help you enjoy every minute of the process. If you think of other Options, Things to Consider, Tips to Save Money, Unique Alternatives, or Questions to Ask, log on to WedSpace.com and search our Questions & Answers section or post a comment on our forum to get answers from wedding professionals and other couples just like you!

If there is anything else you would like to see included in this book, please write to us at: WS Publishing Group; 7290 Navajo Road, Suite 207; San Diego, California 92119. We will include your ideas and suggestions in our next printing. We listen to brides and grooms like you — that is why WS Publishing Group has become the best-selling publisher of wedding planners!

Sincerely,

Elizabeth H. Lluch

Wedding Planning Timeline

This timeline itemizes everything you need to do or consider when planning your wedding and the best timeframe in which to accomplish each activity.

✔ NINE MONTHS & EARLIER

- ❑ Announce your engagement
- ❑ Select a date for your wedding
- ❑ Hire a professional wedding consultant
- ❑ Determine the type of wedding you want:
  - ❊ location
  - ❊ formality
  - ❊ time of day
  - ❊ number of guests, etc.
- ❑ Determine budget and how expenses will be shared
- ❑ Develop a record-keeping system for payments made
- ❑ Consolidate all guest lists: bride's, groom's, bride's family, groom's family, and organize as follows:
  - ❊ those who must be invited
  - ❊ those who should be invited
  - ❊ those who would be nice to invite

NINE MONTHS & EARLIER CONT'D

- ❑ Decide if you want to include children among guests
- ❑ Select and reserve ceremony site
- ❑ Select and reserve your officiant
- ❑ Select and reserve reception site
- ❑ Select and order your bridal gown and headpiece
- ❑ Determine your color scheme
- ❑ Send engagement notice with a photograph to your friends and family
- ❑ Buy a calendar and note all important activities:
  - showers
  - luncheons
  - parties
  - get-togethers, etc.
- ❑ If ceremony or reception is at home, arrange for home or garden improvements as needed
- ❑ Order passport, visa or birth certificate, if needed for your honeymoon or marriage license
- ❑ Select and book photographer
- ❑ Select Maid of Honor, Best Man, bridesmaids and ushers (approx. one usher per 50 guests)

SIX TO NINE MONTHS BEFORE WEDDING

- ❑ Select flower girl and ring bearer
- ❑ Select and book reception musicians or DJ
- ❑ Schedule fittings and delivery dates for yourself, attendants, flower girl and ring bearer
- ❑ Select and book videographer
- ❑ Select and book florist

FOUR TO SIX MONTHS BEFORE WEDDING

- ❑ Start shopping for each other's wedding gifts
- ❑ Reserve rental items needed for ceremony and reception
- ❑ Finalize guest list
- ❑ Select and order wedding invitations, announcements and other stationery such as thank-you notes, wedding programs, and seating cards
- ❑ Address invitations or hire a calligrapher
- ❑ Set date, time and location for your rehearsal dinner
- ❑ Arrange accommodations for out-of-town guests
- ❑ Start planning your honeymoon
- ❑ Select and book all miscellaneous services, i.e. gift attendant, valet parking, etc.
- ❑ Register for gifts
- ❑ Purchase shoes and accessories
- ❑ Begin to break in your shoes

TWO TO FOUR MONTHS BEFORE WEDDING

- ❑ Select bakery and order wedding cake
- ❑ Order party favors
- ❑ Select and order room decorations
- ❑ Purchase honeymoon attire and luggage
- ❑ Select and book transportation for wedding day
- ❑ Check blood test and marriage license requirements
- ❑ Shop for wedding rings and engrave them
- ❑ Consider having your teeth cleaned or bleached
- ❑ Consider writing a will and/or prenuptial agreement

TWO TO FOUR MONTHS BEFORE WEDDING CONT'D

- ❑ Plan activities for your out-of-town guests both before and after the wedding
- ❑ Purchase gifts for wedding attendants

SIX TO EIGHT WEEKS BEFORE WEDDING

- ❑ Mail invitations. Include accommodation choices and a map to assist guests in finding the ceremony and reception sites
- ❑ Maintain a record of RSVPs and all gifts received
- ❑ Send thank-you notes upon receipt of gifts
- ❑ Determine hairstyle and makeup
- ❑ Schedule to have your hair, makeup and nails done the day of the wedding
- ❑ Finalize shopping for wedding day accessories such as toasting glasses, ring pillow, guest book, etc.
- ❑ Set up an area or a table in your home to display gifts as you receive them
- ❑ Have your formal wedding portrait taken
- ❑ Change name and address on drivers license, social security card, insurance policies, subscriptions, bank accounts, memberships, etc.
- ❑ Select and reserve wedding attire for groom, ushers, father of the bride and ring bearer
- ❑ Select a guest book attendant. Decide where and when to have guests sign in
- ❑ Mail invitations to rehearsal dinner
- ❑ Get blood test and health certificate
- ❑ Obtain marriage license

✔ SIX TO EIGHT WEEKS BEFORE WEDDING CONT'D

- ❑ Plan a luncheon or dinner with your bridesmaids. Give them their gifts at that time or at the rehearsal dinner
- ❑ Find "something old, something new, something borrowed, something blue, and a six pence (or shiny penny) for your shoe"
- ❑ Finalize your menu, beverage and alcohol order

✔ TWO TO SIX WEEKS BEFORE WEDDING

- ❑ Confirm ceremony details with your officiant
- ❑ Arrange final fitting of bridesmaids' dresses
- ❑ Have final fitting of your gown and headpiece
- ❑ Finalize rehearsal dinner plans; arrange seating, and write names on place cards, if desired
- ❑ Make final floral selections
- ❑ Make a detailed timeline for your wedding party
- ❑ Make a detailed timeline for your service providers
- ❑ Confirm details with all service providers, including attire. Give them a copy of your wedding timeline
- ❑ Start packing for your honeymoon
- ❑ Finalize addressing and stamping announcements
- ❑ Decide if you want to form a receiving line. If so, determine when and where to form the line
- ❑ Contact guests who haven't RSVP'd
- ❑ Pick up rings and check for fit
- ❑ Meet with photographer and confirm special photos you want

TWO TO SIX WEEKS BEFORE WEDDING CONT'D

- ❑ Meet with videographer and confirm special events or people you want videotaped
- ❑ Meet with musicians and confirm music to be played during special events such as first dance
- ❑ Continue writing thank-you notes as gifts arrive
- ❑ Remind bridesmaids and ushers of when and where to pick up their wedding attire
- ❑ Purchase the lipstick, nail polish and any other accessories you want your bridesmaids to wear
- ❑ Determine ceremony seating for special guests. Give a list to the ushers
- ❑ Plan reception room layout and seating with your reception site manager or caterer
- ❑ Write names on place cards for arranged seating

THE LAST WEEK

- ❑ Pick up wedding attire and make sure everything fits
- ❑ Do final guest count and notify your caterer or reception site manager
- ❑ Arrange for someone to drive the getaway car
- ❑ Review the schedule of events and last-minute arrangements with your service providers
- ❑ Confirm all honeymoon reservations and accommodations. Pick up tickets and travelers checks
- ❑ Finish packing your suitcases for the honeymoon
- ❑ Familiarize yourself with guests' names. It will help during the receiving line and reception

THE LAST WEEK CONT'D

- ❑ Have the post office hold your mail while you are away on your honeymoon

THE REHEARSAL DAY

- ❑ Review list of things to bring to the rehearsal
- ❑ Put suitcases in getaway car
- ❑ Give your bridesmaids the lipstick, nail polish and accessories you want them to wear for the wedding
- ❑ Give Best Man the officiant's fee and any other checks for service providers. Instruct him to deliver these checks the day of the wedding
- ❑ Arrange for someone to bring accessories such as flower basket, ring pillow, guestbook and pen, toasting glasses, cake-cutting knife and napkins to the ceremony and reception
- ❑ Arrange for someone to mail announcements the day after the wedding
- ❑ Arrange for someone to return rental items such as tuxedos, slip and cake pillars after the wedding
- ❑ Provide each member of your wedding party with a detailed schedule of events for the wedding day
- ❑ Review ceremony seating with ushers

THE WEDDING DAY

- ❑ Review list of things to bring to the ceremony
- ❑ Give the groom's ring to the Maid of Honor

THE WEDDING DAY CONT'D

- ❑ Give the bride's ring to the Best Man
- ❑ Simply follow your detailed schedule of events
- ❑ Relax and enjoy your wedding!

OTHER

- ❑ ....
- ❑ ....
- ❑ ....
- ❑ ....
- ❑ ....
- ❑ ....
- ❑ ....
- ❑ ....
- ❑ ....

Wedding Budget

This budget analysis provides you with a break down of all the expenses you can expect to incur in a wedding of any size.

WEDDING BUDGET BREAKDOWN

The following pages will give you an idea of price ranges — how much each detail of the wedding traditionally costs. This will give you a sense of what you can expect to spend for each aspect of the wedding.

Next, estimate the amount of money you will spend on each item in the budget checklist and write that amount in the "Budget" column after each item. The "Actual" column is for you to input your actual expenses as you purchase items or hire your service providers.

PRICE RANGES

CEREMONY

- Ceremony Site Fee .... $100 - $1,000
- Officiant's Fee .... $100 - $500
- Officiant's Gratuity .... $50 - $250
- Guest Book/Pen/Penholder .... $30 - $100
- Ring Bearer Pillow .... $15 - $75
- Flower Girl Basket .... $20 - $75

WEDDING ATTIRE

- Bridal Gown .... $500 - $10,000
- Alterations .... $75 - $500
- Headpiece/Veil .... $60 - $500
- Gloves .... $15 - $100
- Jewelry .... $60 - $2,000
- Garter/Stockings .... $15 - $60
- Shoes .... $50 - $500
- Hairdresser .... $50 - $200 per person
- Makeup Artist .... $30 - $150 per person
- Manicure/Pedicure .... $15 - $75 per person
- Groom's Formal Wear .... $60 - $200

PHOTOGRAPHY

- Bride & Groom's Album .... $900 - $9,000
- Engagement Photograph .... $75 - $300
- Formal Bridal Portrait .... $75 - $300
- Parents' Album .... $100 - $600
- Proofs/Previews .... $100 - $600
- Digital Files .... $100 - $800
- Extra Prints 5x7: $5-20; 8x10: $15-30; 11x14: $30-100

PRICE RANGES

VIDEOGRAPHY

- Main Video ....$600 - $4,000
- Titles ....$50 - $300
- Extra Hours ....$35 - $150 per hour
- Photo Montage ....$60 - $300
- Extra Copies ....$15 - $50

STATIONERY

- Invitations ....$0.75 - $6 each
- Response Cards ....$0.40 - $1 each
- Reception Cards ....$0.40 - $1 each
- Ceremony Cards ....$0.40 - $1 each
- Pew Cards ....$0.25 - $1 each
- Seating/Place Cards ....$0.25 - $1 each
- Rain Cards ....$0.25 - $1 each
- Maps ....$0.50 - $1 each
- Ceremony Programs ....$0.75 - $3 each
- Announcements ....$0.75 - $2 each
- Thank-You Notes ....$0.40 - $0.75 each
- Stamps ....$0.39 - $1 each
- Calligraphy ....$0.50 - $3 each
- Napkins/Matchbooks ....$0.50 - $1.50 each

RECEPTION

- Reception Site Fee ....$300 - $5,000 each
- Hors d'Oeuvres ....$3 - $20 per person
- Main Meal/Caterer ....$20 - $100 per person
- Liquor/Beverages ....$8 - $35 per person
- Bartending/Bar Setup Fee ....$75 - $500

PRICE RANGES

RECEPTION CONT'D

- Corkage Fee....................$5 - $20 per bottle
- Fee to Pour Coffee....................$0.25 - $1 per person
- Service Providers' Meals....................$10 - $30 per person
- Gratuity....................15 - 25% of total food & beverage bill
- Party Favors....................$1 - $5 per person
- Bride & Groom Send-off....................$0.35 - $2 per person
- Gift Attendant....................$20 - $100
- Parking Fee/Valet Services....................$3 - $10 per car

MUSIC

- Ceremony Music....................$100 - $900
- Reception Music....................$500 - $5,000

BAKERY

- Wedding Cake....................$2 - $12 per piece
- Groom's Cake....................$1 - $2 per piece
- Cake Delivery/Setup Fee....................$40 - $100
- Cake-Cutting Fee....................$0.75 - $2.50 per person
- Cake Top....................$20 - $150
- Cake Knife/Toasting Glasses....................$15 - $120/$10 - $100

FLOWERS

Bouquets

- Bride....................$75 - $400
- Tossing....................$20 - $100
- Maid of Honor....................$25 - $100
- Bridesmaids....................$25 - $100

PRICE RANGES

FLOWERS CONT'D

Floral Hairpieces

- Maid of Honor/Bridesmaids....$8 - $100
- Flower Girl....$8 - $75

Corsages

- Bride's Going Away....$10 - $50
- Family Members....$10 - $35

Boutonnieres

- Groom....$4 - $25
- Ushers/Other Family Members....$3 - $15

Ceremony

- Main Altar....$50 - $3,000
- Altar Candelabra....$50 - $200
- Aisle Pews....$5 - $75

Reception

- Reception Site....$300 - $3,000
- Head Table....$100 - $600
- Guest Tables....$10 - $100
- Buffet Table....$50 - $500
- Punch Table....$10 - $100
- Cake Table....$30 - $300
- Cake....$20 - $100
- Cake Knife....$5 - $35
- Toasting Glasses....$10 - $35
- Floral Delivery/Setup Fee....$25 - $200

PRICE RANGES

DECORATIONS

- Table Centerpieces .... $10 - $100 each

TRANSPORTATION

- Transportation .... $35 - $100 per hour

RENTAL ITEMS

- Bridal Slip .... $25 - $75
- Ceremony Accessories .... $100 - $500
- Tent/Canopy .... $300 - $5,000
- Dance Floor .... $100 - $600
- Tables/Chairs .... $3 - $10 per person
- Linen/Tableware .... $3 - $25 per person
- Heaters .... $25 - $75 each
- Lanterns .... $6 - $60 each

GIFTS

- Bride's Gift .... $50 - $500
- Groom's Gift .... $50 - $500
- Bridesmaids' Gifts .... $25 - $200 per gift
- Ushers' Gifts .... $25 - $200 per gift

MISCELLANEOUS

- Newspaper Announcements .... $40 - $100
- Marriage License .... $20 - $100
- Prenuptial Agreement .... $500 - $3,000
- Bridal Gown Preservation .... $100 - $250
- Bridal Bouquet Preservation .... $100 - $500
- Wedding Consultant .... $500 - $10,000
- Wedding Planning Online .... $25 - $200
- Taxes .... approx 7.5% of total wedding budget

✔ MY WEDDING BUDGET	Budget	Actual
TOTAL AMOUNT	$....................	$....................

✔ CEREMONY	Budget	Actual
(Typically = 5% of Budget)	$....................	$....................
❑ Ceremony Site Fee	$....................	$....................
❑ *Officiant's Fee*	$....................	$....................
❑ *Officiant's Gratuity*	$....................	$....................
❑ Guest Book/Pen/Holder	$....................	$....................
❑ Ring Bearer Pillow	$....................	$....................
❑ Flower Girl Basket	$....................	$....................
SUBTOTAL	$....................	$....................

✔ WEDDING ATTIRE	Budget	Actual
(Typically = 10% of Budget)	$....................	$....................
❑ Bridal Gown	$....................	$....................
❑ Alterations	$....................	$....................
❑ Headpiece/Veil	$....................	$....................
❑ Gloves	$....................	$....................
❑ Jewelry	$....................	$....................
❑ Garter/Stockings	$....................	$....................
❑ Shoes	$....................	$....................
❑ Hairdresser	$....................	$....................
❑ Makeup Artist	$....................	$....................

Items in italics are traditionally paid for by the groom or his family.

WEDDING ATTIRE CONT'D

	Item	Budget	Actual
❑	Manicure/Pedicure	$	$
❑	*Groom's Formal Wear*	$	$
	SUBTOTAL	$	$

PHOTOGRAPHY

	Item	Budget	Actual
	(Typically = 9% of Budget)	$	$
❑	Bride & Groom's Album	$	$
❑	Engagement Photograph	$	$
❑	Formal Bridal Portrait	$	$
❑	Parents' Album	$	$
❑	Proofs/Previews	$	$
❑	Digital Files	$	$
❑	Extra Prints	$	$
	SUBTOTAL	$	$

VIDEOGRAPHY

	Item	Budget	Actual
	(Typically = 5% of Budget)	$	$
❑	Main Video	$	$
❑	Titles	$	$
❑	Extra Hours	$	$
❑	Photo Montage	$	$
❑	Extra Copies	$	$
	SUBTOTAL	$	$

Items in italics are traditionally paid for by the groom or his family.

✔ STATIONERY CONT'D	Budget	Actual
(Typically = 4% of Budget)	$....................	$....................
❑ Invitations	$....................	$....................
❑ Response Cards	$....................	$....................
❑ Invitations	$....................	$....................
❑ Response Cards	$....................	$....................
❑ Reception Cards	$....................	$....................
❑ Ceremony Cards	$....................	$....................
❑ Pew Cards	$....................	$....................
❑ Seating/Place Cards	$....................	$....................
❑ Rain Cards	$....................	$....................
❑ Maps	$....................	$....................
❑ Ceremony Programs	$....................	$....................
❑ Announcements	$....................	$....................
❑ Thank-You Notes	$....................	$....................
❑ Stamps	$....................	$....................
❑ Calligraphy	$....................	$....................
❑ Napkins/Matchbooks	$....................	$....................
SUBTOTAL	$....................	$....................

✔ RECEPTION	Budget	Actual
(Typically = 35% of Budget)	$....................	$....................
❑ Reception Site Fee	$....................	$....................
❑ Hors d'Oeuvres	$....................	$....................
❑ Main Meal/Caterer	$....................	$....................
❑ Liquor/Beverages	$....................	$....................

✔	RECEPTION CONT'D	Budget	Actual
❑	Bartending/Bar Setup Fee	$	$
❑	Corkage Fee	$	$
❑	Fee to Pour Coffee	$	$
❑	Service Providers' Meals	$	$
❑	Gratuity	$	$
❑	Party Favors	$	$
❑	Disposable Cameras	$	$
❑	Rose Petals/Rice	$	$
❑	Gift Attendant	$	$
❑	Parking Fee/Valet Services	$	$
	SUBTOTAL	$	$

✔	MUSIC	Budget	Actual
	(Typically = 5% of Budget)	$	$
❑	Ceremony Music	$	$
❑	Reception Music	$	$
	SUBTOTAL	$	$

✔	BAKERY	Budget	Actual
	(Typically = 2% of Budget)	$	$
❑	Wedding Cake	$	$
❑	*Groom's Cake*	$	$

Items in italics are traditionally paid for by the groom or his family.

✔ BAKERY CONT'D	Budget	Actual
❑ Cake Delivery/Setup Fee	$....................	$....................
❑ Cake-Cutting Fee	$....................	$....................
❑ Cake Top	$....................	$....................
❑ Cake Knife	$....................	$....................
❑ Toasting Flutes	$....................	$....................
SUBTOTAL	$....................	$....................

✔ FLOWERS	Budget	Actual
(Typically = 6% of Budget)	$....................	$....................
BOUQUETS		
❑ *Bride*	$....................	$....................
❑ Tossing	$....................	$....................
❑ Maid of Honor	$....................	$....................
❑ Bridesmaid	$....................	$....................
FLORAL HAIRPIECES		
❑ Maid of Honor	$....................	$....................
❑ Bridesmaids	$....................	$....................
❑ Flower Girl	$....................	$....................
CORSAGES		
❑ *Bride's Going Away*	$....................	$....................
❑ *Family Members*	$....................	$....................
BOUTONNIERES		
❑ *Groom*	$....................	$....................

FLOWERS CONT'D

		Budget	Actual
	BOUTONNIERES CONT'D		
❑	Ushers	$	$
❑	Family Members	$	$
	CEREMONY SITE		
❑	Main Altar	$	$
❑	Altar Candelabra	$	$
❑	Aisle Pews	$	$
	RECEPTION SITE		
❑	Head Table	$	$
❑	Guest Tables	$	$
❑	Buffet Table	$	$
❑	Punch Table	$	$
❑	Cake Table	$	$
❑	Cake	$	$
❑	Cake Knife	$	$
❑	Toasting Glasses	$	$
❑	Floral Delivery/Setup Fee	$	$
	SUBTOTAL	$	$

DECORATIONS

		Budget	Actual
	(Typically = 3% of Budget)	$	$
❑	Table Centerpieces	$	$
❑	Balloons	$	$
	SUBTOTAL	$	$

TRANSPORTATION

	Budget	Actual
(Typically = 2% of Budget)	$....................	$....................
❑ Transportation	$....................	$....................
SUBTOTAL	$....................	$....................

RENTAL ITEMS

	Budget	Actual
(Typically = 3% of Budget)	$....................	$....................
❑ Bridal Slip	$....................	$....................
❑ Ceremony Accessories	$....................	$....................
❑ Tent/Canopy	$....................	$....................
❑ Dance Floor	$....................	$....................
❑ Tables/Chairs	$....................	$....................
❑ Linen/Tableware	$....................	$....................
❑ Heaters	$....................	$....................
❑ Lanterns	$....................	$....................
❑ Other Rental Items	$....................	$....................
SUBTOTAL	$....................	$....................

GIFTS

	Budget	Actual
(Typically = 3% of Budget)	$....................	$....................
❑ *Bride's Gift*	$....................	$....................
❑ Groom's Gift	$....................	$....................

Items in italics are traditionally paid for by the groom or his family.

GIFTS CONT'D

	Budget	Actual
❑ Bridesmaids' Gifts	$	$
❑ *Ushers' Gifts*	$	$
SUBTOTAL	$	$

PARTIES

	Budget	Actual
(Typically = 4% of Budget)	$	$
❑ Bridesmaids' Luncheon	$	$
❑ *Rehearsal Dinner*	$	$
SUBTOTAL	$	$

MISCELLANEOUS

	Budget	Actual
(Typically = 4% of Budget)	$	$
❑ Announcements	$	$
❑ *Marriage License*	$	$
❑ *Prenuptial Agreement*	$	$
❑ Gown Preservation	$	$
❑ Bouquet Preservation	$	$
❑ Wedding Consultant	$	$
❑ Wedding Planning Online	$	$
❑ Taxes	$	$
SUBTOTAL	$	$

GRAND TOTAL	$	$

Items in italics are traditionally paid for by the groom or his family.

Ceremony

Your ceremony is a reflection of who you are. It can be as simple or as elaborate as you desire.

CEREMONY VENUE

Many people choose to have a traditional ceremony in a church, while others have taken their special day outdoors to a park or the beach. These days, anything goes!

OPTIONS

- Church
- Cathedral
- Chapel
- Temple
- Synagogue
- Private home
- Garden
- Hotel
- Club
- Restaurant
- Hall
- Park
- Museum
- Art gallery
- Yacht
- Winery
- Beach

THINGS TO CONSIDER

- Formality of your wedding
- Season
- Number of guests
- Religious affiliation
- Restrictions or guidelines regarding photography, videography, music, decorations, candles, and rice or rose petal-tossing
- Proximity of the ceremony site to the reception site
- Parking availability
- Handicapped accessibility
- Time constraints

TIPS TO SAVE MONEY

- Have your ceremony at the same facility as your reception to save a second rental fee
- Set a realistic guest list and stick to it
- Hire an experienced wedding consultant
- At a church or temple, ask if there is another wedding that day and share the cost of floral decorations with that bride
- Membership in a church, temple, or club can reduce rental fees
- At a garden wedding, have guests stand and omit the cost of renting chairs

OFFICIANT'S FEE/GRATUITY

The officiant's fee is the fee paid to the person who performs your wedding ceremony.

OPTIONS

- Priest
- Clergyman
- Minister
- Pastor
- Chaplain
- Rabbi
- Judge
- Justice of the Peace

THINGS TO CONSIDER

- Consider also including a gratuity. The officiant's gratuity is a discretionary amount of money given to the officiant in addition to the fee.
- Some officiants may not accept a fee or gratuity, depending on your relationship with him or her. If a fee is refused, send a donation to the officiant's church or synagogue.
- The groom puts this fee in a sealed envelope and gives it to his Best Man or wedding consultant, who gives it to the officiant either before or immediately after the ceremony.

UNIQUE ALTERNATIVES

- Have a friend or loved one become certified as an officiant

REMEMBER!

- Your officiant and his or her partner should be invited to your reception, so don't forget to include them on your guest list and seating chart

CEREMONY READINGS

Incorporate readings into your ceremony.

POPULAR READINGS

- Beatitudes
- Corinthians 13:1-13
- Ecclesiastes 3:1-9
- Ephesians 3:14-19; 5:1-2
- Genesis 1:26-28
- Genesis 2:4-9, 15-24
- Hosea 2:19-21
- Isaiah 61:10I
- John 4:7-16
- John 15:9-12, 17:22-24
- Mark 10:6-9
- Proverbs 31:10-31
- Romans 12:1-2, 9-18
- Ruth 1:16-17
- Tobit 8:56-58

UNIQUE ALTERNATIVES

- Excerpts from *The Prophet* by Kahlil Gibran
- *The Alchemist* by Paulo Coelho
- *The Velveteen Rabbit* by Margery Williams Bianco
- Poems by Pablo Neruda
- Shakespeare's Sonnets
- Song lyrics

THE GUEST BOOK

The guest book is a formal register that your guests sign as they arrive at the ceremony or reception. It serves as a memento of who attended your wedding.

THINGS TO CONSIDER

- A traditional guest book is an album of blank pages or photos of the couple with space around the edges for guests to write their names and a message
- Have more than one pen in case one runs out of ink
- If you are planning a large ceremony (over 300 guests), consider having more than one book and pen so that your guests don't have to wait to sign in

UNIQUE ALTERNATIVES

- For a wishing tree, provide a small potted tree and a basket of small cards with a loop of ribbon or string. Guests write loving wishes on the cards and hang them on the tree. The bride and groom keep the wishes and plant the tree wherever they would like to have a special reminder of their wedding day

- Set out a Polaroid camera and have guests snap photos of each other, then provide a permanent marker for them write a note on the photo frame

RING BEARER PILLOW

The ring bearer, usually a boy between the ages of 4 and 8, carries the bride and groom's rings or mock rings on a pillow. He follows the Maid of Honor and precedes the flower girl or bride in the processional.

THINGS TO CONSIDER

- Ring pillows will come with a ribbon tie or may be a small box to keep rings secure. You can find them at most gift shops and bridal boutiques.

- Purchase a handmade pillow from sites like Etsy.com. Many sellers will allow you to customize the ring pillow with colors that match your wedding.

UNIQUE ALTERNATIVES

- Consider using a beautiful box or other meaningful receptacle in place of a traditional ring pillow. Ideas might include a jewelry box from your mother, a large seashell to complement a beach theme, or a dish from a loved one's home

FLOWER GIRL BASKET

The flower girl carries a basket filled with flowers, rose petals, or paper rose petals to scatter as she walks down the aisle. She follows the ring bearer or Maid of Honor and precedes the bride during the processional.

THINGS TO CONSIDER

- Flower girl baskets come in many styles and colors. You can find them at most florists, gift shops, and bridal boutiques
- Ask your florist if you can borrow a basket and attach a pretty white bow to it to save money
- Discuss any restrictions regarding rose petal, flower, or paper-tossing with your ceremony site
- Select a basket which complements your guest book and ring bearer pillow

UNIQUE ALTERNATIVES

- Have the flower girl carry a small bouquet instead of a flower basket
- Give the flower girl a small purse you choose especially for her in place of a basket and let her keep it after the wedding

NOTES

WEDDING VOWS

Jot down ideas for your wedding vows below:

PERSONALIZED WEDDING VOWS

QUESTIONS TO ASK ABOUT THE CEREMONY SITE

Bring this list of questions with you when looking at possible ceremony sites. Use the information to compare and contrast different locations.

BE SURE TO ASK

- What is the website and e-mail of the ceremony site?

Option 1 ....

Option 2 ....

- What is the address of the ceremony site?

Option 1 ....

Option 2 ....

- What is the name of my contact person?

Option 1 ....

Option 2 ....

- What is the phone number of my contact person?

Option 1 ....

Option 2 ....

- What dates & times are available?

Option 1 ....

Option 2 ....

BE SURE TO ASK CONT'D

- Do vows need to be approved?

Option 1 ....

Option 2 ....

- What is the ceremony site fee?

Option 1 ....

Option 2 ....

- What is the payment policy?

Option 1 ....

Option 2 ....

- What is the cancellation policy?

Option 1 ....

Option 2 ....

- Does the facility have liability insurance?

Option 1 ....

Option 2 ....

- What is the minimum and maximum number of guests allowed?

Option 1 ....

Option 2 ....

BE SURE TO ASK CONT'D

- What is the denomination, if any, of the facility?

Option 1 ....

Option 2 ....

- What restrictions are there with regards to religion?

Option 1 ....

Option 2 ....

- Is an officiant available? At what cost?

Option 1 ....

Option 2 ....

- Are outside officiants allowed?

Option 1 ....

Option 2 ....

- Are any musical instruments available for our use?

Option 1 ....

Option 2 ....

- If so, what is the fee?

Option 1 ....

Option 2 ....

- What music restrictions are there, if any?

Option 1 ....

Option 2 ....

BE SURE TO ASK CONT'D

- What photography restrictions are there, if any?

Option 1 ....

Option 2 ....

- What videography restrictions are there, if any?

Option 1 ....

Option 2 ....

- Are there are any restrictions for rice/petal-tossing?

Option 1 ....

Option 2 ....

- Are candlelight ceremonies allowed?

Option 1 ....

Option 2 ....

- What floral decorations are available/allowed?

Option 1 ....

Option 2 ....

- When is my rehearsal to be scheduled?

Option 1 ....

Option 2 ....

- Is there handicap accessibility and parking?

Option 1 ....

Option 2 ....

BE SURE TO ASK CONT'D

- How many parking spaces are available for my wedding party?

Option 1 ....

Option 2 ....

- Where are they located?

Option 1 ....

Option 2 ....

- How many parking spaces are available for my guests?

Option 1 ....

Option 2 ....

- What rental items are necessary?

Option 1 ....

Option 2 ....

- What is the fee?

Option 1 ....

Option 2 ....

- Other:

Option 1 ....

Option 2 ....

CEREMONY INFORMATION

Use this form to organize the information on your ceremony site after you have made your final selection.

CEREMONY AT-A-GLANCE

- Ceremony Site: ....
- Contact Person: ....
- Website: ....
- Email: ....
- City: ....
- State/Zip Code: ....
- Phone Number: ....
- Hours: ....
- Payment Policy: ....
- Cancellation Policy: ....
- Setup Time: ....
- Tear Down Time: ....
- Notes: ....

  ....

  ....

  ....

CEREMONY READING SELECTIONS

Use this form to organize your ceremony reading selections.

CEREMONY READINGS

- Source: ....
  Selection: ....
  Read by: ....
  When: ....
- Source: ....
  Selection: ....
  Read by: ....
  When: ....
- Source: ....
  Selection: ....
  Read by: ....
  When: ....
- Source: ....
  Selection: ....
  Read by: ....
  When: ....

✽ Source: ....

Selection: ....

Read by: ....

When: ....

✽ Source: ....

Selection: ....

Read by: ....

When: ....

✽ Source: ....

Selection: ....

Read by: ....

When: ....

✽ Source: ....

Selection: ....

Read by: ....

When: ....

✽ Source: ....

Selection: ....

Read by: ....

When: ....

THINGS TO DO

- ❑
- ❑
- ❑
- ❑
- ❑

NOTES

Attire

Every bride wants to look her very best on her wedding day. This takes more than just a great dress. It takes knowing what looks best on your body and knowing how to maximize your assets.

BRIDAL GOWN

Bridal gowns come in a wide variety of styles, materials, colors, lengths, and prices. In selecting your gown, keep in mind the time of year and formality of your wedding.

GOWN STYLES

✻ **A-Line/Princess:** Fitted around the bodice and flows out to the ground, resembling the outline of an uppercase A. Flattering on almost all body types.

GOWN STYLES CONT'D

* **Empire:** Raised waistline sits just below the bust; the rest of the dress flows down to the hem. Accentuates a small bust or can hide a long torso, short legs, or a pear-shaped figure.

* **Column or Sheath:** A narrow shape that flows straight down from the neckline to the hem. Tends to hug the body and show any and all of your curves; best worn by lean figures.

* **Ball Gown:** This traditional style pairs a fitted bodice with a full skirt. Ideal for slender or pear-shaped figures and accentuates the waistline.

* **Mermaid:** Contours to the body from the chest to the knee, then flares out to the hem. A sexy look that highlights the curves of a woman's body, thus confidence is a must.

GOWN FEATURES

NECKLINES

When it comes to finding the right neckline, there are many options to choose from, depending on the statement you want to make. Each neckline will influence the overall look of your gown in a different way, so you want to be sure you know your options.

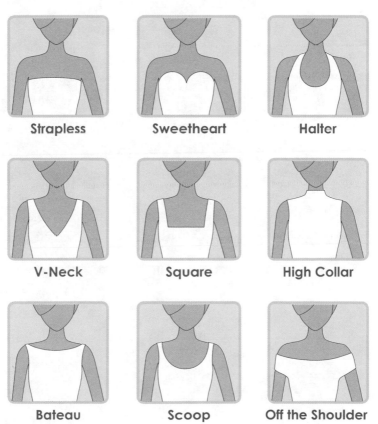

Strapless

Sweetheart

Halter

V-Neck

Square

High Collar

Bateau

Scoop

Off the Shoulder

GOWN FEATURES CONT'D

SLEEVES

The second element that influences your overall style is the sleeve length. When considering sleeves for your wedding dress, you will want to keep in mind the time of day and the season in which you will be married.

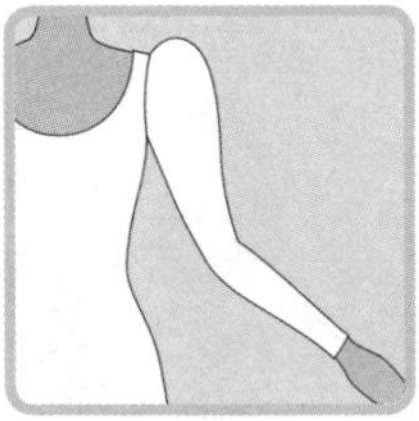

Balloon

Poet

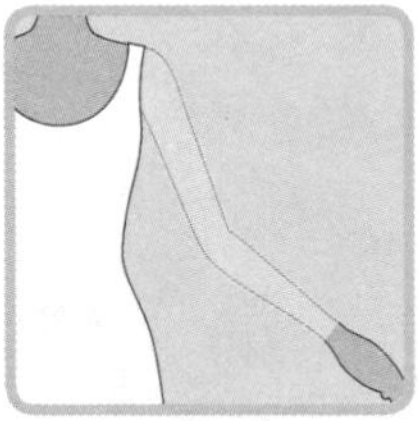

Illusion

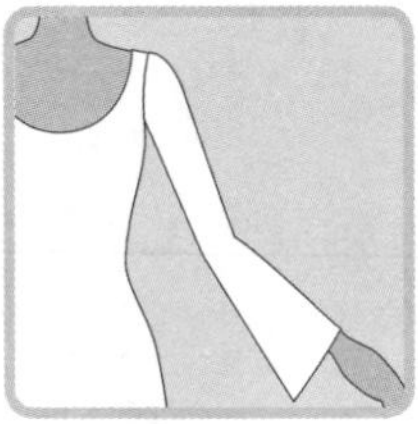

Bell

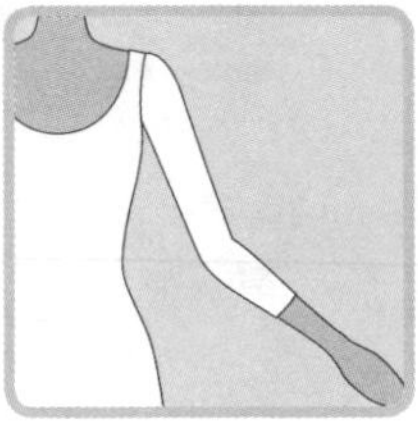

3/4 Length

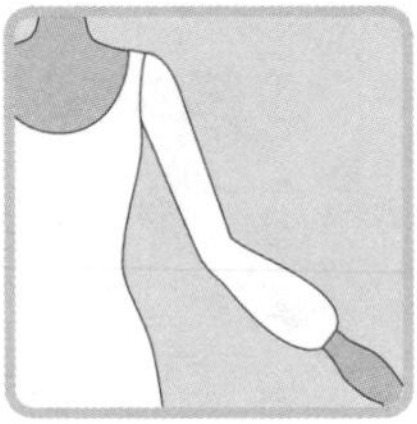

Bishop

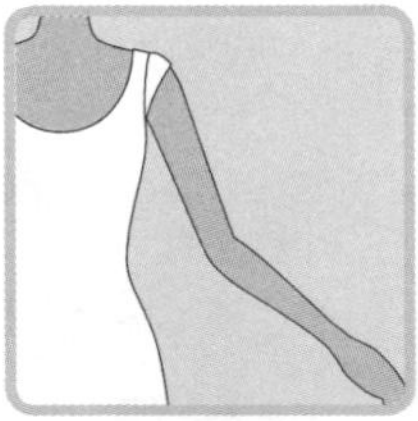

Capped

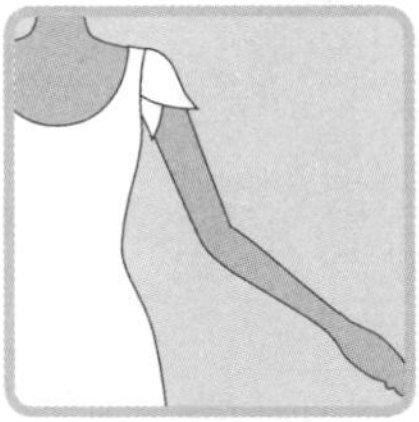

Petal

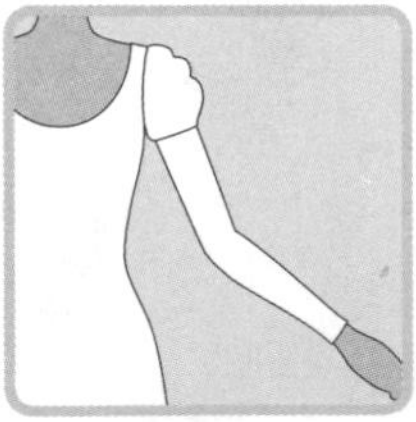

Juliet

GOWN FEATURES CONT'D

TRAIN

The formality of your wedding, more than any other factor, should influence your decision to have a train.

The length of your train should be consistent with the location and time of your wedding.

Brush

Court

Chapel

Cathedral

Royal

Watteau

UNIQUE ALTERNATIVES

- Try a tea-length hem – one that falls just below the knee or mid-calf. Shorter gowns are perfect for less formal ceremonies, vintage themes, and outdoor weddings

- A full skirt on a shorter gown also gives the bride beautiful shape and gives the dress movement

- Add a colored sash or shoe

- Brides are going so far as to wear a colored wedding gown. Pink, blue, gold, red, and even gray hues

AT THE BRIDAL SALON

- Always call and make an appointment before stopping in
- Bring your mother, sister, Maid of Honor, or Mother-in-Law along with you
- Bring something to tie your hair back with, a strapless bra, and a shoe with a heel about the height of what you will wear on your Big Day
- Have some idea of what you want and bring in tear sheets from magazines; however, be open to trying on styles you hadn't considered
- Discuss your budget with the salesperson up front so she doesn't waste time bringing you gowns far out of your price range

AT THE BRIDAL SALON CONT'D

- Wear a little makeup; trying on a wedding gown with a bare face is like trying on an evening gown with sneakers
- Bring a camera and have someone take pictures of you in each dress, from different angles
- Try on many different styles. You never know how a cut will look on you until you put it on
- Try on different veil lengths with different gowns
- Ask the salesperson to recommend the right undergarments for each style you try on. Once you select a dress, you will need to buy the proper undergarments to wear to each of your fittings
- Discuss what change or alterations you might want and how much they each cost
- Be sure you can move, walk, sit, and dance freely in the dress you choose
- If you are pregnant, be sure you find a bridal salon that is willing to work with your changing shape and size in the months leading up to the wedding
- Decide if you want or need a bustle and, if so, have the salesperson show your mother or Maid of Honor how to bustle your gown

REMEMBER!

- Don't forget to ask when your gown will arrive, and be sure to get this in writing. The gown should arrive at least six weeks before the wedding so you can have it tailored and select the appropriate accessories

TIPS TO SAVE MONEY

- Ask about discontinued styles and gowns. Watch for clearances and sales, or buy your gown "off the rack"

- Shop for a secondhand gown. Get recommendations from brides and bridal bloggers to find a reputable store or online shop. Designer gowns for sale secondhand have usually been worn for less than 6 hours, and many never even been worn at all (a wedding may have been canceled or the bride changed her mind about the dress at the last minute). Always ask questions about the quality of a secondhand gown, request photos, and pay with a credit card

- Restore or refurbish a family heirloom gown. Or, if you have a friend, sister, or other family member who is planning a wedding, consider purchasing a gown that you could both wear. Change the accessories to personalize it

- Buy a wedding dress that's not a "wedding dress." Look for dresses from designers' non-wedding lines. This is especially doable if you're interested in a less traditional gown. You will often find gorgeous gowns with beautiful beading, lace, and detailing that are less than $500 simply because they aren't labeled as "wedding" dresses

- Some gown manufacturers suggest ordering a size larger than needed. Save money by finding an independent tailor specializing in bridal gown alterations

DRESS FITTINGS

- First fitting: 6 months before
- Second fitting: 1 month before
- Final fitting: 1 to 3 weeks before
- Wear the proper undergarments, shoes, and accessories to each fitting
- Ask how to care for your dress, i.e. what to do if it gets a spot or wrinkles
- Walk, sit, and even dance in your dress to be sure you are comfortable with how it fits and moves
- Look for wrinkling, puckering, gapping, bulging, pulling at the seams, or any other issues that indicate problems with the fit

REMEMBER!

- Don't bite your tongue! Your wedding gown should be everything you want, aside from the fact that it is a very large financial investment. Speak up if you spot a problem or there is something that isn't up to par
- Have as many fittings as it takes to get the dress right

VEIL & HEADPIECE

After you have found the perfect dress, you will want to complete your perfect look with a few finishing accessories.

OPTIONS FOR VEILS

- **Blusher:** Single layer veil that is worn over the face during the ceremony, and then flipped back over the head

- **Fingertip:** The most common veil length, reaching to the fingertips, and can be worn with a variety of dress styles

- **Birdcage:** A vintage look, made of lace or French netting, that covers the face

- **Ballet or Waltz:** Long veil flows from the headpiece down to the ankles; a good option for a dress without a train

- **Mantilla:** Spanish-inspired veil drapes over the head and is usually made of lace

OPTIONS FOR VEILS CONT'D

- **Pouf:** Gathered material at the point where it connects to the headpiece, creating added volume

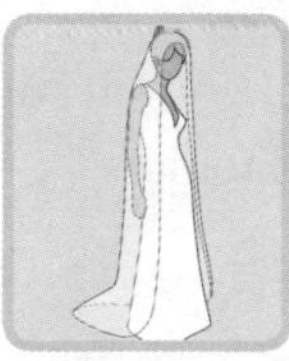

- **Chapel:** A formal look, extending 2½ yards from the headpiece, flowing down over the train of the dress

- **Cathedral:** The most formal veil, it extends 3½ yards from the headpiece

THINGS TO CONSIDER

- Veils come in different styles and lengths. Select a length that complements the length of your train
- Consider the total look you're trying to achieve with your gown, headpiece, veil, and hairstyle
- If possible, schedule your hair "test appointment" the day you go veil shopping—you'll be able to see how your veil looks with your hairstyle

 OPTIONS FOR HEADPIECES

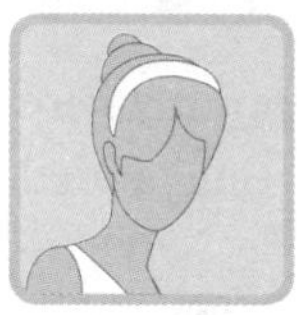

- **Headband:** Can be made from satin, lace, or the same material as your dress

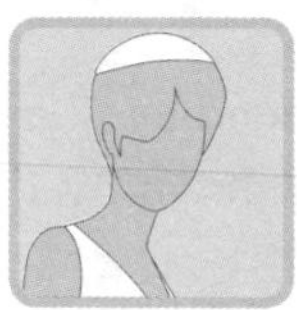

- **Juliet Cap:** Sits on the crown of your head; generally adorned with pearls or beading

- **Snood:** Encases the bun at the back of your head with beading, lace, or crystal adornments. Add a veil to this look by attaching it to the bottom of the headpiece

- **Hairpins:** Adorn wedding hair with pearls, crystals, flowers, butterflies and more

- **Wreath:** Ask your florist to create this headpiece for you using greenery or the same flowers from your bouquet

- **Tiara:** A popular headpiece that sits across the top of your head. A great headpiece if you want to feel like a princess on your big day

OPTIONS FOR HEADPIECES CONT'D

- **Profile:** An ornamental comb that can accent a sophisticated updo, such as a French twist or chignon. Profiles are generally worn without a veil

- **Garden Hat:** Wide-brimmed hat that makes a dramatic statement, especially well suited for an outdoor summer wedding

- **Crown:** Similar to the tiara in style, the crown extends all the way around in a full circle that sits atop your head

- **Pins:** Can be adorned with a variety of things, from pearls and crystals, to flowers and butterflies. Great in any type of updo or gently swept-back hair

REMEMBER!

- Some boutiques offer a free headpiece or veil with the purchase of a gown. Ask in advance

- Headpieces are commonly used as the anchor for your veil, holding it in place for the entire event or allowing for the detachment of the veil through the use of hooks, snaps, or Velcro

GLOVES

There are a variety of options, from wrist length gloves that cover just your hands to opera length gloves that reach above your elbows. You can choose from a number of fabrics that provide different looks, from classic satin to romantic lace.

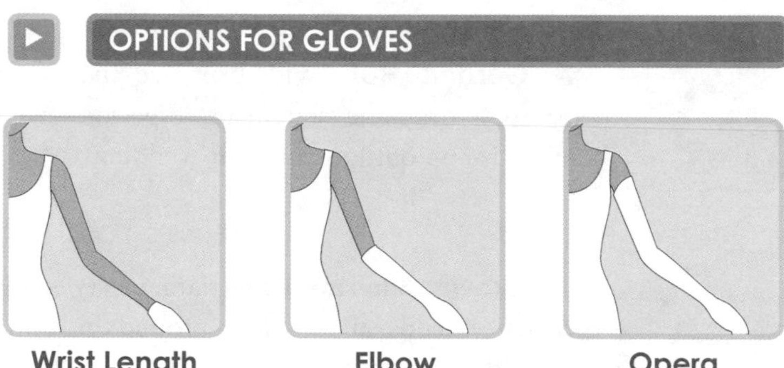

Wrist Length | Elbow | Opera

SHOES

The shoes you choose to wear will also affect your overall look. Be sure to stay consistent with the formality of your gown.

Flat | Ballet Slipper | Low Heel

OPTIONS FOR SHOES

Mary Jane

Mule

Sandal

Wedge

Platform

Pump

Stacked Heel

Stiletto

Slingback

THINGS TO CONSIDER

- Break in your wedding shoes a few weeks in advance
- Have your shoes picked out before you go to your first fitting so the hem of your dress can be adjusted to the appropriate length
- Consider two pairs of shoes, one for the ceremony and photos, and a second for dancing during the reception

ADDITIONAL ACCESSORIES

Additional accessories to purchase or rent:

Slip

- Full/half slip
- Petticoat

Garter/Stockings

- It is traditional to wear a garter just above the knee for the garter toss
- Select stockings with care, especially if the groom will be removing your garter at the reception
- Consider having your Maid of Honor carry an extra pair of stockings in case you get a run

Handbag

- Choose something small and discreet such as a clutch to hold items such as lip gloss, tissues and mints

Jewelry

- Select pieces of jewelry that can be classified as "something old, something new, something borrowed, or something blue"
- Purchase complementary jewelry for your bridesmaids for a coordinated look

Undergarments

- Thong, body slimmer, bustier, lingerie, etc.

ADDITIONAL ACCESSORIES CONT'D

Something Old

- Represents the history of the bride and ties her to her family

Something New

- Represents the future and the bride's ties to her new family

Something Borrowed

- Something borrowed should come from someone who is happily married and is carried in the hopes that their good fortune may rub off on you

Something Blue

- Blue is the color of purity and is carried to represent faithfulness in the marriage

GUIDELINES

The guidelines below will help you select the most appropriate gown for your wedding.

Informal wedding

- Street-length gown
- Corsage or small bouquet

Semiformal wedding

- Floor-length gown
- Chapel train
- Fingertip veil
- Small bouquet

Formal daytime wedding

- Floor-length gown
- Chapel or sweep train
- Fingertip veil or hat
- Gloves
- Medium-sized bouquet

Formal evening wedding

- Same as formal daytime except longer veil

Very formal wedding

- Floor-length gown
- Cathedral train
- Full-length veil
- Long sleeves or long arm-covering gloves
- Cascading bouquet

QUESTIONS FOR A BRIDAL BOUTIQUE

Use these questions to compare and contrast different bridal boutiques.

BE SURE TO ASK

- What is the boutique name?

Option 1 ....

Option 2 ....

- What is the website/email address?

Option 1 ....

Option 2 ....

- What is the name of my contact person?

Option 1 ....

Option 2 ....

- What is the phone number of my contact person?

Option 1 ....

Option 2 ....

- What are your hours? Are appointments needed?

Option 1 ....

Option 2 ....

- Do you offer any discounts or giveaways?

Option 1 ....

Option 2 ....

BE SURE TO ASK CONT'D

- What major bridal gown lines do you carry?

Option 1 ....

Option 2 ....

- Do you carry outfits for the mother of the bride?

Option 1 ....

Option 2 ....

- Do you carry bridesmaids gowns and/or tuxedos?

Option 1 ....

Option 2 ....

- Do you carry outfits for the flower girl/ring bearer?

Option 1 ....

Option 2 ....

- What is the cost of the desired bridal gown?

Option 1 ....

Option 2 ....

- What is the cost of the desired headpiece?

Option 1 ....

Option 2 ....

- Do you offer in-house alterations?

Option 1 ....

Option 2 ....

BE SURE TO ASK CONT'D

✼ If so, what are your fees?

Option 1 ....

Option 2 ....

✼ Do you carry bridal shoes?

Option 1 ....

Option 2 ....

✼ What is their price range?

Option 1 ....

Option 2 ....

✼ Do you dye shoes to match outfits?

Option 1 ....

Option 2 ....

✼ Do you rent bridal slips?

Option 1 ....

Option 2 ....

✼ If so, what is the rental fee?

Option 1 ....

Option 2 ....

✼ What is the estimated date of delivery for my gown?

Option 1 ....

Option 2 ....

BE SURE TO ASK CONT'D

- What is your payment policy?

Option 1 ....

Option 2 ....

- What is your cancellation policy?

Option 1 ....

Option 2 ....

- Other ....

Option 1 ....

Option 2 ....

- Other ....

Option 1 ....

Option 2 ....

- Other ....

Option 1 ....

Option 2 ....

- Other ....

Option 1 ....

Option 2 ....

- Other ....

Option 1 ....

Option 2 ....

BRIDAL ATTIRE CHECKLIST

- ❑ Full Slip
- ❑ Garter
- ❑ Gloves
- ❑ Gown
- ❑ Handbag
- ❑ Headpiece/hat
- ❑ Jewelry
- ❑ Lingerie
- ❑ Panty Hose
- ❑ Petticoat or Slip
- ❑ Shoes
- ❑ Something Old
- ❑ Something New
- ❑ Something Borrowed
- ❑ Something Blue
- ❑ Veil

GROOM'S ATTIRE

The groom should select his attire based on the formality of the wedding. The most popular colors are black, white, and gray.

GUIDELINES

Use the following guidelines to select customary attire for the groom:

Informal wedding

- Business suit
- White dress shirt and tie

Semi-formal daytime

- Formal suit
- White dress shirt
- Cummerbund or vest
- Four-in-hand or bow tie

GUIDELINES CONT'D

Semi-formal evening

- Formal suit or dinner jacket
- Matching trousers
- White shirt
- Cummerbund or vest
- Black bow tie
- Cuff links and studs

Formal daytime

- Cutaway or stroller jacket
- Waistcoat
- Striped trousers
- White wing-collared shirt
- Striped tie
- Studs and cuff links

Formal evening

- Black dinner jacket
- Matching trousers
- Waistcoat
- White tuxedo shirt
- Bow tie
- Cummerbund or vest
- Cuff links

Very formal daytime

- Cutaway coat
- Wing-collared shirt
- Ascot
- Striped trousers
- Cuff links and gloves

GUIDELINES CONT'D

Very formal evening

- Formal suit or dinner jacket
- Matching trousers
- White shirt
- Cummerbund or vest
- Black bow tie
- Cuff links and studs

THINGS TO CONSIDER

- Keep in mind the formality of your wedding, the time of day, and the bride's gown
- Consider darker colors for a fall or winter wedding and lighter colors for a spring or summer wedding
- Reserve tuxedos for yourself and your ushers several weeks before the wedding to ensure a wide selection and to allow enough time for alterations
- Plan to pick up the tuxedos a few days before the wedding to allow time for last-minute alterations in case they don't fit properly
- Out-of-town men in your wedding party can be sized at any tuxedo shop. They can send their measurements to you or directly to the shop where you are going to rent your tuxedos

THINGS TO CONSIDER CONT'D

- Ask about the store's return policy and be sure you delegate to the appropriate person (usually your Best Man) the responsibility of returning all tuxedos within the time allotted

TIPS TO SAVE MONEY

- Try to negotiate getting your tuxedo for free or at a discount in exchange for having your father, your fiancé's father, and ushers rent their tuxedos at that shop

BEAUTY

The right makeup, hair, and nail color will give you a beautiful look and style. Each aspect of wedding-day beauty should complement the others; thus, having trial run-throughs is very important.

HAIRDRESSER

- Have your professional hairdresser experiment with your hair and headpiece before your wedding day so there are no surprises
- Most hairdressers will include the cost of a sample session in your package. Ask in advance
- Write down the specifics of each style so that things go quickly and smoothly on your wedding day

HAIRDRESSER CONT'D

- On the big day, you can go to the salon or have the stylist meet you at your home or dressing site
- Consider having him/her arrange your bridal party's hair for a consistent look
- Negotiate having your hair arranged free of charge or at a discount in exchange for bringing your mother, your fiancé's mother, and your bridal party to the salon

MAKEUP

- A professional makeup artist will apply makeup that should last throughout the day
- Consider a trial run before the day of the wedding so there are no surprises
- Have him/her apply makeup for your mother, your fiancé's mother, and your bridesmaids for a consistent look
- Make sure he or she has been trained in makeup for photography. It is very important to wear the proper amount of makeup for photographs
- Consider having your makeup trial right before your hairdresser trial — that way you'll see how your hair looks with your makeup on

MAKEUP CONT'D

- Negotiate having your makeup applied free of charge or at a discount in exchange for bringing your mother, your fiancé's mother, and your wedding party to the salon
- Ask for samples to use for touch-ups during your wedding

MANICURE/PEDICURE

- As a final touch, it's nice to have a professional manicure and/or pedicure the day of your wedding
- Don't forget to bring the appropriate color nail polish with you for your appointment
- Consider having the manicurist give your mother, your fiancé's mother, and your bridesmaids a manicure in the a complementary color
- Make this a fun occasion where you can bond with your bridal party

Photography

The photographs taken at your wedding are the best way to preserve your special day. Chances are, you and your fiancé will look at the photos many times during your life together.

BRIDE & GROOM'S ALBUM

Hiring a good photographer is one of the most important tasks in planning your wedding.

CHOOSING A PHOTOGRAPHER

- Ask to look at albums that the photographer has ready to be delivered, or proofs of weddings recently photographed

- Study each photographer's style. Some photographers are known for formal poses, while others specialize in more candid, creative shots. Some can do both

CHOOSING A PHOTOGRAPHER CONT'D

- Ask for references, but keep in mind photographers will obviously give you names of clients who they know are pleased with their work. (Why give a name of someone who wasn't?)
- When comparing prices, compare the quantity and size of the photographs in your album and the type of album that each photographer will use
- Ask how many photos will be taken on average at a wedding of your size
- Some photographers do not work with a DVD of proofs. Rather, they simply supply you with a finished album after the wedding. Doing this may reduce the cost of your album but will also reduce your selection of photographs
- Compare at least three photographers for quality, value, and price. Photographers who shoot weddings "on the side" are usually less expensive, but the quality of their photographs may not be as good
- Ask for specials and package deals
- Discuss your shot list
- Negotiate! If you are up front about your budget for photography and tell a vendor you really want to find a way to work together, they will negotiate with you

CHOOSING A PHOTOGRAPHER CONT'D

- Find out the rules and present them to your photographer so he is knowledgeable about your site; some churches do not allow photographs to be shot during the ceremony

REMEMBER!

- Make sure the photographer you interview is the specific person who will photograph your wedding and that someone else isn't going to show up on your Big Day. Reputable companies will make sure that you meet with (and view the work of) the photographer who will actually photograph your wedding. This way you can get an idea of his or her style and personality and begin to establish a rapport with your photographer

- Your chosen photographer's name should go on your contract!

TIPS TO SAVE MONEY

- Hire a professional photographer for the formal shots of your ceremony only. Rely on guests to take candid shots with their personal cameras and have them upload them to an online photo gallery you set up

ENGAGEMENT PHOTOS

Many couples are interested in a set of engagement photos to accompany their wedding-day photography. These make a nice keepsake for the couple, as well as a gift for friends and family.

THINGS TO CONSIDER

- Consider hiring the same photographer for engagement photos as for the wedding; many will build the price into the total photography package
- Decide whether you want candid shots or posed portrait shots or a combination of both
- Many couples prefer to have engagement photos taken outside and not in a studio; ask your photographer if he or she can scout locations
- Engagement shoots can include more than one wardrobe change. Bring outfits with bright colors and do not wear prints or white, which do not photograph as nicely
- Wear nice shoes, as many shots will be full-body
- Engagement shoots usually include affectionate shots such as the couple hugging or even kissing, so talk to your partner about what you're both comfortable with
- Ask your photographer to take some classic bridal portraits (shots of just bride)

PARENTS' ALBUM

The parents' album is a smaller version of the bride and groom's album that is given to each set of parents as a gift.

THINGS TO CONSIDER

- Ask to see samples of different types of parents' albums available
- Ask if the albums can be personalized with your names and the date of the wedding on the front cover
- As if the photographer can create coffee table-style books from the digital files
- Try to negotiate at least one free parents' album with the purchase of the bride and groom's album

PROOFS & PREVIEWS

Proof DVDs are the preliminary prints or digital images from which the bride and groom select photographs for their album and for their parents' albums.

THINGS TO CONSIDER

- When selecting a package, ask how many photos the photographer will take. The more images, the wider the selection you will have to choose from

THINGS TO CONSIDER CONT'D

- For a wide selection, the photographer must take at least 3 to 5 times the number of prints that will go into your album
- Ask the photographer how soon after the wedding you will get your proofs. Request this in writing. Ideally, the proofs will be ready by the time you get back from your honeymoon
- Ask your photographer to use your proofs as part of your album package to save developing costs

DIGITAL FILES

Digital files allow you to view your photos on a screen in a large size with lots of detail. A photographer will provide your digital proofs to you on a DVD.

THINGS TO CONSIDER

- Ask if your photographer is shooting with a professional digital camera that can create extra-large file sizes, which is important for clarity, if you want very large prints made (such as 24" by 30")
- Most photographers will not sell you the digital files up front since they hope to make a profit on selling extra prints after the wedding

THINGS TO CONSIDER CONT'D

- Ask the photographers you interview how long they keep the files and at what point they will become available to you. A professional photographer should keep a back-up copy of the digital files for at least 10 years

- Many photographers will sell you the entire set of digital files after all photos have been ordered by family and friends

REMEMBER!

- Once you own your digital files, make a back-up copy of your disk every 5 or 6 years, as CDs and DVDs can deteriorate after 8 years or so

TIPS TO SAVE MONEY

- If you can wait, consider contacting the photographer a few years later and ask if he or she will sell you the files at that time. Most photographers will be glad to sell them at a bargain price

EXTRA PRINTS

Extra prints are photographs ordered in addition to the main album or parents' albums. These are usually purchased as gifts for the bridal party, close friends and family members.

THINGS TO CONSIDER

- It is important to discuss the cost of extra prints with your photographer since prices vary considerably. Knowing what extra prints will cost ahead of time will help you know if the photographer is truly within your budget
- Think how many extra prints you would like to order and figure this into your budget before selecting a photographer

TIPS TO SAVE MONEY

- If you can wait, consider not ordering any reprints during the first few years after the wedding. A few years later, contact the photographer and ask if he or she will sell you the files for a discounted price

QUESTIONS FOR A PHOTOGRAPHER

Use these questions to compare and contrast different photographers you are interested in hiring.

BE SURE TO ASK

- What is the company/photographer name?

Option 1 ....

Option 2 ....

- What is the website of the photographer?

Option 1 ....

Option 2 ....

- What is the email of the photographer?

Option 1 ....

Option 2 ....

- What is the phone number of my contact person?

Option 1 ....

Option 2 ....

- How many years of experience do you have?

Option 1 ....

Option 2 ....

- Who will be the photographer at my wedding?

Option 1 ....

Option 2 ....

BE SURE TO ASK CONT'D

- What percentage of your business is dedicated to weddings?

Option 1 ....

Option 2 ....

- Approximately how many weddings have you photographed?

Option 1 ....

Option 2 ....

- Will you bring an assistant with you to my wedding?

Option 1 ....

Option 2 ....

- How do you typically dress for weddings?

Option 1 ....

Option 2 ....

- Do you have a professional studio?

Option 1 ....

Option 2 ....

- What type of equipment do you use?

Option 1 ....

Option 2 ....

BE SURE TO ASK CONT'D

* Do you bring backup equipment with you to weddings?

Option 1 ....

Option 2 ....

* Do you need to visit the ceremony and reception sites prior to the wedding?

Option 1 ....

Option 2 ....

* Do you have liability insurance?

Option 1 ....

Option 2 ....

* Are you skilled in diffused lighting and soft focus?

Option 1 ....

Option 2 ....

* Can you take studio portraits?

Option 1 ....

Option 2 ....

* Can you retouch my images?

Option 1 ....

Option 2 ....

BE SURE TO ASK CONT'D

- Can digital files be purchased? If so, what is the cost?

Option 1 ....

Option 2 ....

- What is the cost of the package I am interested in?

Option 1 ....

Option 2 ....

- What is your payment policy?

Option 1 ....

Option 2 ....

- What is your cancellation policy?

Option 1 ....

Option 2 ....

- Do you offer a money-back guarantee?

Option 1 ....

Option 2 ....

- Do you use DVD proofing?

Option 1 ....

Option 2 ....

- How many photographs will I have to choose from?

Option 1 ....

Option 2 ....

BE SURE TO ASK CONT'D

❊ When will I get my proofs?

Option 1 ....

Option 2 ....

❊ When will I get my album?

Option 1 ....

Option 2 ....

❊ What is the cost of an engagement portrait?

Option 1 ....

Option 2 ....

❊ What is the cost of a formal bridal portrait?

Option 1 ....

Option 2 ....

❊ What is the cost of a parents' album?

Option 1 ....

Option 2 ....

❊ What is the cost of a groom's album?

Option 1 ....

Option 2 ....

❊ What is the cost of a 5" x 7" reprint?

Option 1 ....

Option 2 ....

BE SURE TO ASK CONT'D

- What is the cost of an 8" x 10" reprint?

Option 1 ....

Option 2 ....

- What is the cost of an 11" x 14" reprint?

Option 1 ....

Option 2 ....

- What is the cost per additional hour of shooting?

Option 1 ....

Option 2 ....

- Other..

Option 1 ....

Option 2 ....

- Other..

Option 1 ....

Option 2 ....

- Other..

Option 1 ....

Option 2 ....

- Other..

Option 1 ....

Option 2 ....

PHOTOGRAPHER INFORMATION

Use this form to organize the information on photographers and photography sessions.

PHOTOGRAPHER AT-A-GLANCE

- Company Name: ....
- Contact Person: ....
- Website: ....
- Email: ....
- Address: ....
- City: ....
- State/Zip Code: ....
- Phone Number: ....
- Payment Policy: ....
- Cancellation Policy: ....
- Notes: ....

....

....

....

....

....

PHOTOGRAPHY SESSIONS AT-A-GLANCE

Engagement Portrait

- Date & Time:
- Location:
- Address:
- City/State/Zip:

Bridal Portrait

- Date & Time:
- Location:
- Address:
- City/State/Zip:

Ceremony

- Date & Time:
- Location:
- Address:
- City/State/Zip:

Reception

- Date & Time:
- Location:
- Address:
- City/State/Zip:

PHOTOGRAPHY SHOT LIST

Discuss with your partner and your photographer what photos must be included on your shot list for your wedding day.

PRE-CEREMONY PHOTOGRAPHS

- ❑ Bride leaving her house
- ❑ Wedding rings with the invitation
- ❑ Bride getting dressed for the ceremony
- ❑ Bride looking at her bridal bouquet
- ❑ Maid of Honor putting garter on bride's leg
- ❑ Bride by herself
- ❑ Bride with her mother
- ❑ Bride with her father
- ❑ Bride with mother and father
- ❑ Bride with her entire family and/or any combination thereof
- ❑ Bride with her Maid of Honor
- ❑ Bride with her bridesmaids
- ❑ Bride with the flower girl and/or ring bearer
- ❑ Bride's mother putting on her corsage
- ❑ Groom leaving his house
- ❑ Groom putting on his boutonniere
- ❑ Groom with his mother
- ❑ Groom with his father
- ❑ Groom with mother and father
- ❑ Groom with his entire family and/or any combination thereof
- ❑ Groom with his Best Man
- ❑ Groom with his ushers
- ❑ First look — when groom first sees the bride

PRE-CEREMONY PHOTOGRAPHS CONT'D

- ❑ Groom with the bride's father
- ❑ Bride and her father getting out of the limousine
- ❑ Special members of the family being seated
- ❑ Groom waiting for the bride before the processional
- ❑ Bride and her father just before the processional

ADDITIONAL PRE-CEREMONY PHOTOGRAPHS

- ❑ ....
- ❑ ....
- ❑ ....
- ❑ ....

CEREMONY PHOTOGRAPHS

- ❑ The processional
- ❑ Bride and groom saying their vows
- ❑ Bride and groom exchanging rings
- ❑ Groom kissing the bride at the altar
- ❑ The recessional

ADDITIONAL CEREMONY PHOTOGRAPHS

- ❑ ....
- ❑ ....
- ❑ ....
- ❑ ....

POST-CEREMONY PHOTOGRAPHS

- ❑ Bride and groom
- ❑ Newlyweds with both of their families
- ❑ Newlyweds with thc entire wedding party
- ❑ Bride and groom signing the marriage certificate
- ❑ Flowers and other decorations

ADDITIONAL POST-CEREMONY PHOTOGRAPHS

- ❑ ....
- ❑ ....
- ❑ ....
- ❑ ....

RECEPTION PHOTOGRAPHS

- ❑ Entrance of newlyweds and wedding party into the reception site
- ❑ Receiving line
- ❑ Guests signing the guest book
- ❑ Toasts
- ❑ First dance
- ❑ Bride and her father dancing
- ❑ Groom and his mother dancing
- ❑ Bride dancing with groom's father
- ❑ Groom dancing with bride's mother
- ❑ Wedding party and guests dancing
- ❑ Cake table
- ❑ Cake-cutting ceremony

RECEPTION PHOTOGRAPHS CONT'D

- ❑ Couple feeding each other cake
- ❑ Buffet table and its decoration
- ❑ Bouquet-tossing ceremony
- ❑ Garter-tossing ceremony
- ❑ Musicians
- ❑ The wedding party table
- ❑ The family tables
- ❑ Candid shots of your guests
- ❑ Bride and groom saying good-bye to their parents
- ❑ Bride and groom looking back, waving goodbye in the getaway car

ADDITIONAL RECEPTION PHOTOGRAPHS

- ❑ ....
- ❑ ....
- ❑ ....
- ❑ ....

OTHER PHOTOGRAPHS

- ❑ ....
- ❑ ....
- ❑ ....
- ❑ ....

Videography

Next to your photo album, videography is the best way to preserve your wedding memories. Unlike photographs, videography captures the mood of the wedding day in motion and sound.

VIDEOGRAPHY

Videography can help capture every beautiful and special moment of your wedding day.

OPTIONS

- A documentary video records your wedding day as it happened, in real time. Very little editing or embellishment is involved. These types of videos are normally less expensive and can be delivered within days after the wedding

- The cinematic type production is more reminiscent of a movie. Most good cinematic wedding videos are shot with two cameras. This type of video requires more time due to the extensive editing of the footage

OPTIONS CONT'D

- Decide if you want music, slow motion, black and white scenes, or other special features in your video

- Decide if you want your video shot in high definition, which delivers a sharper picture

THINGS TO CONSIDER

- Be sure to hire a videographer who specializes in weddings and ask to see samples of his or her work. Weddings are very specialized events

- Look at previous weddings the videographer has done, a notice the color and brightness of the screen, as well as the quality of sound. This will indicate the quality of his or her equipment

- Note whether the picture is smooth or jerky. This will indicate the videographer's skill level

- Ask about special effects such as titles, dissolve, and multiple screens. Find out what's included in the cost of your package so that there are no surprises at the end!

- If you are getting married in a church, find out the church's policies regarding videography. Some churches might require the videographer to film the ceremony from a specific distance

THINGS TO CONSIDER CONT'D

- Find out how much your videographer would charge to stay longer than the contracted time. Do this in case your reception lasts longer than expected. Don't forget to get this fee in writing
- Ask your videographer what the charge is for extra copies
- Before making your own copies of your wedding video, check with your videographer; many contracts prohibit it, and doing so could be copyright infringement
- Ask about creating a photo montage, which is a series of photographs set to music on video
- As in photography, be sure to have in your contract the videographer who will actually shoot your wedding, so someone else doesn't show up on your Big Day

TIPS TO SAVE MONEY

- The most expensive is not necessarily the best. The videographer who uses one camera (instead of multiple cameras) is usually the most cost effective and may be all you need
- Consider hiring a company that offers both videography and photography. You might save money by combining the two services

TIPS TO SAVE MONEY CONT'D

- To reduce the amount of time you'll need to use the videographer, consider recording the ceremony only
- There are many websites that allow you to create your own photo montage either for free or at a very low price. You can then transfer your photo montage to a DVD
- Ask a family member or close friend to videotape your wedding. However, realize that without professional equipment and expertise, the final product may not be quite as polished

QUESTIONS FOR A VIDEOGRAPHER

Use these questions to compare and contrast different videographers you are interested in hiring.

BE SURE TO ASK

- What is your company name?

Option 1 ....

Option 2 ....

- What is your website?

Option 1 ....

Option 2 ....

- What is your e-mail?

Option 1 ....

Option 2 ....

- What is your address?

Option 1 ....

Option 2 ....

- How many years of experience do you have?

Option 1 ....

Option 2 ....

- How many weddings have you recorded?

Option 1 ....

Option 2 ....

BE SURE TO ASK CONT'D

- Are you the person who will videotape my wedding?

Option 1 ....

Option 2 ....

- Will you bring an assistant with you to my wedding?

Option 1 ....

Option 2 ....

- What type of equipment do you use?

Option 1 ....

Option 2 ....

- Do you have a wireless microphone?

Option 1 ....

Option 2 ....

- Do you bring backup equipment with you?

Option 1 ....

Option 2 ....

- Do you visit the location before the wedding?

Option 1 ....

Option 2 ....

- Do you edit the tape after the event?

Option 1 ....

Option 2 ....

BE SURE TO ASK CONT'D

❊ Who keeps the raw footage and for how long?

Option 1 ....

Option 2 ....

❊ When will I receive the final product?

Option 1 ....

Option 2 ....

❊ What is the cost of the desired package?

Option 1 ....

Option 2 ....

❊ What does it include?

Option 1 ....

Option 2 ....

❊ Can you make a photo montage? What is your price?

Option 1 ....

Option 2 ....

❊ What is your payment policy?

Option 1 ....

Option 2 ....

❊ What is your cancellation policy?

Option 1 ....

Option 2 ....

VIDEOGRAPHER INFORMATION

Use this form to organize the information on your final videographer selection.

VIDEOGRAPHER AT-A-GLANCE

- Company Name:
- Contact Person:
- Website:
- Email:
- Address:
- City:
- State/Zip Code:
- Phone Number:
- Payment Policy:
- Cancellation Policy:
- Notes:

Stationery

Begin creating your guest list as soon as possible. Ask your parents and the groom's parents for a list of people they would like to invite in addition to your own list. Make sure names and addresses are current.

INVITATIONS

After you make your guest list, you will need to decide on the type, style, colors, and format of your invitations.

 OPTIONS

- There are three types of invitations: traditional/formal, contemporary, and informal
- The traditional/formal wedding invitation is white, soft cream, or ivory with raised black lettering. The printing is done on the top page of a double sheet of thick paper; the inside is left blank

OPTIONS CONT'D

- The contemporary invitation is typically an individualized presentation that makes a statement about the bride and groom

- Informal invitations are often printed on the front of a single, heavyweight card and may be handwritten or preprinted

- There are three types of printing: engraved, thermography, and offset printing

- Engraving is the most expensive, traditional, and formal type of printing. It also takes the longest to complete

- Thermography is a process that fuses powder and ink to create a raised letter. This takes less time than engraving and is less expensive

- Offset printing, the least expensive, is the quickest to produce and offers a variety of styles and colors. It is also the least formal

- You may address the invitations yourself, hire a professional calligrapher, or have your invitations addressed using calligraphy by computer

- Make sure you use the same method or person to address both the inner and outer envelopes

- Calligraphy is a form of elegant handwriting often used to address invitations for formal occasions

THINGS TO CONSIDER

- Begin creating your guest list as soon as possible
- Ask your parents and the groom's parents for a list of people they would like to invite. You and your fiancé should make your own lists
- Make certain that all names are spelled correctly and that all addresses are current
- Traditional wedding invitations should be addressed in black or blue fountain pen
- Determine if you wish to include children; if so, add their names to your list
- All children over the age of 16 should receive their own invitation
- Order your invitations at least four months before the wedding. Allow an additional month for engraved invitations
- Order approximately 20 percent more stationery than your actual count
- Remember that oversized envelopes will require additional postage
- Allow a minimum of two weeks to address and mail the invitations, longer if using a calligrapher or if your guest list is very large

THINGS TO CONSIDER CONT'D

- Consider ordering invitations to the rehearsal dinner, as these should be in the same style as the wedding invitation
- Invitations are traditionally issued by the bride's parents; but if the groom's parents are assuming some of the wedding expenses, the invitations should be in their names also
- If all your guests are to be invited to both the ceremony and the reception, a combined invitation may be sent without separate enclosure cards
- Order one invitation for each married or cohabiting couple that you plan to invite
- The officiant and his or her spouse, as well as your attendants, should receive an invitation
- Mail all invitations at the same time, six to eight weeks before the wedding
- Order commemorative stamps for your postage!

TIPS TO SAVE MONEY

- Thermography looks like engraving and is one-third of the cost
- Choose paper stock that is reasonable and yet achieves your overall look

TIPS TO SAVE MONEY CONT'D

- Select invitations that can be mailed using just one stamp
- Take a short course to learn the art of calligraphy so that you can address your own invitations
- If you have a computer with a laser printer, you can address the invitations yourself using one of many beautiful calligraphy fonts
- Order at least 25 extra invitations in case you ruin some or add people to your list. To reorder this small number of invitations later would cost nearly three times the amount you'll spend up front

SAMPLES OF TRADITIONAL/FORMAL INVITATIONS

- **When the bride's parents sponsor the wedding:**

Mr. and Mrs. Alexander Waterman Smith
request the honor of your presence
at the marriage of their daughter
Carol Ann
to
Mr. William James Clark
on Saturday, the fifth of August
two thousand eight
at two o'clock in the afternoon
Saint James by-the-Sea
La Jolla, California

SAMPLES OF TRADITIONAL/FORMAL INVITATIONS

When the groom's parents sponsor the wedding:

Mr. and Mrs. Michael Burdell Clark
request the honor of your presence
at the marriage of
Miss Carol Ann Smith
to their son
Mr. William James Clark

When both the bride and groom's parents sponsor the wedding:

Mr. and Mrs. Alexander Waterman Smith
and
Mr. and Mrs. Michael Burdell Clark
request the honor of your presence
Miss Carol Ann Smith
to
Mr. William James Clark

OR

Mr. and Mrs. Alexander Waterman Smith
request the honor of your presence
at the marriage of their daughter
Carol Ann Smith
to
William James Clark
son of Mr. and Mrs. Michael Burdell Clark

SAMPLES OF TRADITIONAL/FORMAL INVITATIONS

- **When the bride and groom sponsor their own wedding:**

The honor of your presence is requested
at the marriage of
Miss Carol Ann Smith
and
Mr. William James Clark

OR

Miss Carol Ann Smith
and
Mr. William James Clark
request the honor of your presence
at their marriage

- **With divorced parents:**

a) When the bride's mother is sponsoring the wedding and is not remarried:

Mrs. Julie Hurden Smith
requests the honor of your presence
at the marriage of her daughter
Carol Ann

SAMPLES OF TRADITIONAL/FORMAL INVITATIONS

b) When the bride's mother is sponsoring the wedding and has remarried:

Mrs. Julie Hurden Booker
requests the honor of your presence
at the marriage of her daughter
Carol Ann Smith

OR

Mr. and Mrs. John Thomas Booker
request the honor of your presence
at the marriage of Mrs. Booker's daughter
Carol Ann Smith

c) When the bride's father is sponsoring the wedding and has not remarried:

Mr. and Mrs. Alexander Waterman Smith
request the honor of your presence
at the marriage of Mr. Smith's daughter
Carol Ann

- **With deceased parents:**
  a) When a close friend or relative sponsors the wedding:

Mr. and Mrs. Brandt Elliott Lawson
request the honor of your presence
at the marriage of their granddaughter
Carol Ann Smith

SAMPLES OF TRADITIONAL/FORMAL INVITATIONS

In military ceremonies, the rank determines the placement of names:

a) Any title lower than sergeant should be omitted. Only the branch of service should be included under that person's name:

Mr. and Mrs. Alexander Waterman Smith
request the honor of your presence
at the marriage of their daughter
Carol Ann
to
William James Clark
United States Army

b) Junior officers' titles are placed below their names and are followed by their branch of service:

Mr. and Mrs. Alexander Waterman Smith
request the honor of your presence
at the marriage of their daughter
Carol Ann
to
William James Clark
First Lieutenant, United States Army

SAMPLES OF TRADITIONAL/FORMAL INVITATIONS

c) If the rank is higher than lieutenant, titles are placed before names, and the branch of service is placed on the following line:

Mr. and Mrs. Alexander Waterman Smith
request the honor of your presence
at the marriage of their daughter
Carol Ann
to
Captain William James Clark
United States Navy

SAMPLES OF CONTEMPORARY INVITATIONS

Mr. and Mrs. Alexander Waterman Smith
would like you to
join with their daughter
Carol Ann
and
William James Clark
in the celebration of their marriage

ADDRESSING INVITATIONS

There are proper ways to address the inner and outer envelopes for your invitations, based on the recipient's age and marital status.

THINGS TO CONSIDER

- Start addressing your invitations at least three months before your wedding, and preferably four months if you are using calligraphy or if your guest list is above 200
- You may want to ask your Maid of Honor or bridesmaids to help you with this time-consuming task, as this is traditionally part of their responsibilities
- If you are working with a wedding consultant, he or she can also help you address invitations
- Organize a luncheon or late afternoon get-together with hors d'oeuvres and make a party out of addressing the envelopes
- The inner envelope is placed unsealed inside the outer envelope, with the flap away from the person inserting
- The invitation and all enclosures are placed inside the inner envelope facing the back flap
- The inner envelope contains the name (or names) of the person (or people) who are invited to the ceremony and/or reception

THINGS TO CONSIDER CONT'D

- The address is not included on the inner envelope
- The outer envelope contains the name (or names) and address of the person (or people) to whom the inner envelope belongs

ADDRESSING INVITATIONS SAMPLES

Note: Inner envelope does not include first names or addresses. The outer envelope includes first names and addresses.

- **Husband and Wife (with same surname)**

  Inner Envelope: Mr. and Mrs. Smith

  Outer Envelope: Mr. and Mrs. Thomas Smith
  (use middle name, if known)

- **Husband and Wife (with different surnames)**

  Inner Envelope: Ms. Banks and Mr. Smith
  (wife first)

  Outer Envelope: Ms. Anita Banks
  Mr. Thomas Smith
  (wife's name & title above husband's)

- **Husband and Wife (wife has professional title)**

  Inner Envelope: Dr. Smith and Mr. Smith
  (wife first)

  Outer Envelope: Dr. Anita Smith
  Mr. Thomas Smith
  (wife's name & title above husband's)

ADDRESSING INVITATIONS SAMPLES CONT'D

Husband and Wife (with children under 16)

Inner Envelope: Mr. and Mrs. Smith
John, Mary, and Glen
(in order of age)

Outer Envelope: Mr. and Mrs. Thomas Smith

Single Woman (regardless of age)

Inner Envelope: Miss/Ms. Smith

Outer Envelope: Miss/Ms. Beverly Smith

Single Woman and Guest

Inner Envelope: Miss/Ms. Smith
Mr. Jones (or "and Guest")

Outer Envelope: Miss/Ms. Beverly Smith

Single Man

Inner Envelope: Mr. Jones
(Master for a young boy)

Outer Envelope: Mr. William Jones

Single Man and Guest

Inner Envelope: Mr. Jones
Miss/Ms. Smith (or "and Guest")

Outer Envelope: Mr. William Jones

Unmarried Couple Living Together

Inner Envelope: Mr. Knight and Ms. Orlandi
(names listed alphabetically)

Outer Envelope: Mr. Michael Knight
Ms. Paula Orlandi

ADDRESSING INVITATIONS SAMPLES CONT'D

Two Sisters (over 16)

Inner Envelope: The Misses Smith
Outer Envelope: The Misses Mary and Jane Smith (in order of age)

Two Brothers (over 16)

Inner Envelope: The Messrs. Smith
Outer Envelope: The Messrs. John and Glen Smith (in order of age)

Brothers & Sisters (over 16)

Inner Envelope: Mary, Jane, John & Glen (name the girls first, in order of age)
Outer Envelope: The Misses Smith
The Messrs. Smith
(name the girls first)

A Brother and Sister (over 16)

Inner Envelope: Jane and John (name the girl first)
Outer Envelope: Miss Jane Smith and Mr. John Smith (name the girl first)

Widow

Inner Envelope: Mrs. Smith
Outer Envelope: Mrs. William Smith

ADDRESSING INVITATIONS SAMPLES CONT'D

- **Divorcee**

  Inner Envelope: Mrs. Smith

  Outer Envelope: Mrs. Jones Smith (maiden name and former husband's surname)

RESPONSE CARDS

Response cards are enclosed with the invitation to determine the number of people who will be attending your wedding.

THINGS TO CONSIDER

- Include a self-addressed and stamped return envelope to make it easy for your guests to return the response cards
- You should not include a line that reads "number of persons" on your response cards because only those whose names appear on the inner and outer envelopes are invited
- Each couple, each single person, and all children over the age of 16 should receive their own invitation
- Indicate on the inner envelope if they may bring an escort or guest
- The omitting of children's names from the inner envelope infers that the children are not invited

SAMPLES OF WORDING FOR RESPONSE CARDS

- M______________________
(The M may be eliminated from the line,
especially if many Drs. are invited)
___ accepts
___ regrets
Saturday the fifth of July
Oceanside Country Club

OR

- The favor of your reply is requested
by the twenty-second of May
M_________________________
will ________ attend

RECEPTION CARDS

If the guest list for the ceremony is larger than that for the reception, a separate card with the date, time and location for the reception should be enclosed with the ceremony invitation.

THINGS TO CONSIDER

- Reception cards should be placed in front of the invitation, facing the back flap and the person inserting them

- You may also include a reception card in all your invitations if the reception is to be held at a different site than the ceremony

TIPS TO SAVE MONEY

- If all people invited to the ceremony are also invited to the reception, include the reception information on the invitation and eliminate the reception card. This will save printing and postage costs

SAMPLES OF RECEPTION CARD WORDING

- **Formally Worded:**

Mr. and Mrs. Alexander Waterman Smith
request the pleasure of your company
Saturday, the third of July
at three o'clock
Oceanside Country Club
2020 Waterview Lane
Oceanside, California

- **Less Formally Worded:**

Reception immediately following the ceremony
Oceanside Country Club
2020 Waterview Lane
Oceanside, California

PEW CARDS

Pew cards may be used to let special guests and family members know they are to be seated in the reserved section on either the bride's side or the groom's side. These are most typically seen in large, formal ceremonies.

OPTIONS

- Pew cards may indicate a specific pew number if specific seats are assigned, or may read "Within the Ribbon" if certain pews are reserved, but no specific seat is assigned

THINGS TO CONSIDER

- Pew cards may be inserted along with the invitation, or may be sent separately after the RSVPs have been returned

- It is often easier to send pew cards after you have received all RSVPs so you know how many reserved pews will be needed

TIPS TO SAVE MONEY

- Include the pew card with the invitation to special guests and just say, "Within the Ribbon." After you have received all your RSVPs, you will know how many pews need to be reserved. This will save you the cost of mailing the pew cards separately

SEATING/PLACE CARDS

Seating and place cards are used to let guests know where they should be seated at the reception.

THINGS TO CONSIDER

- Select a traditional or contemporary design for your place cards, depending on the style of your wedding
- Place cards should be laid out alphabetically on a table at the entrance to the reception. Each card should correspond to a table—either by number, color, or other identifying factor. Each table should be marked accordingly
- Regardless of the design, place cards must contain the same information: the bride and groom's names on the first line; the date on the second line; the third line is left blank for you to write in the guest's name; and the fourth line is for the table number, color, or other identifying factor

MAPS

Maps to the ceremony and/or reception are becoming frequent inserts in wedding invitations.

THINGS TO CONSIDER

- Maps should be printed in the same style as the invitation and are usually on a small, heavier card
- Maps should include both written and visual instructions, keeping in mind the fact that guests may be coming from different locations

THINGS TO CONSIDER CONT'D

- If maps are not printed in the same style or on the same type of paper as the invitation, they should be mailed separately
- Order extra maps to hand out at the ceremony if the reception is at a different location

TIPS TO SAVE MONEY

- Purchase or download software that allows you to design your own maps
- Have your ushers hand out maps to the reception after the ceremony
- Have a wedding website that includes interactive maps

CEREMONY PROGRAMS

Ceremony programs show the sequence of events and tell guests who your attendants, officiant, and ceremony musicians are.

OPTIONS

- Ceremony programs can be handed out by the ushers, or they can be placed at the back of the church for guests to take as they enter

SAMPLE CEREMONY PROGRAM

The Marriage of
Carol Ann Smith and William James Clark
the eleventh of March, 2008
San Diego, California

OUR CEREMONY

Prelude:
All I Ask of You, by Andrew Lloyd Webber

Processional:
Canon in D Major, by Pachelbel

Rite of Marriage

Welcome guests

Statement of intentions

Marriage vows

Exchange of rings

Blessing of bride and groom

Pronouncement of marriage

Presentation of the bride and groom

Recessional:
Trumpet Voluntary, by Jeromiah Clarke

SAMPLE CEREMONY PROGRAM CONT'D

OUR WEDDING PARTY

Maid of Honor:
Susan Smith, Sister of Bride

Best Man:
Brandt Clark, Brother of Groom

Bridesmaids:
Janet Anderson, Friend of Bride
Lisa Bennett, Friend of Bride

Ushers:
Mark Gleason, Friend of Groom
Tommy Olson, Friend of Groom

Officiant:
Father Henry Thomas

OUR RECEPTION

Please join us after the ceremony
in the celebration of our marriage at:
La Valencia Hotel
1132 Prospect Street
La Jolla, California

ANNOUNCEMENTS

Announcements may be sent to friends who are not invited to the wedding because the number of guests must be limited or because they live too far away. They may also be sent to acquaintances who, while not particularly close to the family, might still wish to know about the marriage.

Announcements are also appropriate for friends and acquaintances who are not expected to attend and for whom you do not want to give an obligation of sending a gift.

THINGS TO CONSIDER

- Announcements should never be sent to anyone who has received an invitation to the ceremony or the reception
- They should include the day, month, year, city, and state where the ceremony took place
- They should be addressed before the wedding and mailed the day of or the day after the ceremony

THANK-YOU NOTES

Regardless of whether the bride has thanked the donor in person or not, she must write a thank-you note for every gift received.

THINGS TO CONSIDER

- Order thank-you notes along with your other stationery at least four months before your wedding

THINGS TO CONSIDER CONT'D

- You should order some with your maiden initials for thank-you notes sent before the ceremony, and the rest with your married initials for notes sent after the wedding and for future use
- Send thank-you notes within two weeks of receiving a gift that arrives before the wedding, and within two months after the honeymoon for gifts received on or after your wedding day
- Be sure to mention the gift you received in the body of the note and let the person know how much you like it and what you plan to do with it

NAPKINS & MATCHBOOKS

Napkins and matchbooks may also be ordered from your stationer. These are placed around the reception room as decorative items and mementos of the event.

THINGS TO CONSIDER

- Napkins and matchbooks can be printed in your wedding colors, or simply white with gold or silver lettering
- Include both of your names and the wedding date
- Consider including a phrase or thought, or a small graphic design above your names

STATIONERY WORDING

Invitations:

STATIONERY WORDING

Announcements:

Reception Cards:

STATIONERY WORDING

Response Cards:

Seating/Place Cards:

Napkins & Matchbooks:

QUESTIONS FOR A STATIONER

Use these questions to compare and contrast different stationers you are interested in using.

BE SURE TO ASK

- What is your company name?

Option 1 ....

Option 2 ....

- What is your website?

Option 1 ....

Option 2 ....

- What is your e-mail?

Option 1 ....

Option 2 ....

- What is your address?

Option 1 ....

Option 2 ....

- How many years of experience do you have?

Option 1 ....

Option 2 ....

- What lines of stationery do you carry?

Option 1 ....

Option 2 ....

BE SURE TO ASK CONT'D

- What types of printing processes do you offer?

Option 1 ....

Option 2 ....

- How soon in advance should I place my order?

Option 1 ....

Option 2 ....

- What is the turnaround time?

Option 1 ....

Option 2 ....

- What is the cost of the desired invitation?

Option 1 ....

Option 2 ....

- What is the cost of the desired announcements?

Option 1 ....

Option 2 ....

- What is the cost of the desired response card?

Option 1 ....

Option 2 ....

- What is the cost of the desired reception card?

Option 1 ....

Option 2 ....

BE SURE TO ASK CONT'D

- What is the cost of the desired thank-you note?

Option 1 ....

Option 2 ....

- What is the cost of the desired wedding program?

Option 1 ....

Option 2 ....

- What is the cost of napkins & matchbooks?

Option 1 ....

Option 2 ....

- What is the cost of addressing in calligraphy?

Option 1 ....

Option 2 ....

- What is your payment policy?

Option 1 ....

Option 2 ....

- What is your cancellation policy?

Option 1 ....

Option 2 ....

- Other..

Option 1 ....

Option 2 ....

STATIONERY INFORMATION

Use this form to organize the information on your final stationery selection.

STATIONERY AT-A-GLANCE

- Company Name:
- Contact Person:
- Website:
- Email:
- Address:
- City:
- State/Zip Code:
- Phone Number:
- Payment Policy:
- Cancellation Policy:
- Notes:

STATIONERY SELECTION

Note details such as paper, style, color, font, and printing.

STATIONERY CHECKLIST

- ❑ Invitations:..
- ❑ Envelopes:...
- ❑ Response Cards/Envelopes:...
- ❑ Reception Cards:..
- ❑ Ceremony Cards:..
- ❑ Pew Cards:..
- ❑ Seating/Place Cards:...
- ❑ Rain Cards:..
- ❑ Maps Cards:..
- ❑ Ceremony Programs:...
- ❑ Announcements:...
- ❑ Thank-You Notes:...
- ❑ Napkins/Matchbooks:...
- ❑ Stamps: ....
- ❑ Other: ....

Reception

The reception is the party where all your guests come together to celebrate your new life as a married couple. The decor and style should reflect and complement your ceremony.

THE RECEPTION SITE

The selection of a reception site will depend on its availability, price, proximity to the ceremony site, and the number of people it will accommodate.

OPTIONS

- Some sites will charge a per person fee that includes the facility, food, tables, silverware, china, and so forth. Examples: hotels, restaurants, and catered yachts
- Other types of sites charge for beverages, linens, and possibly tables and chairs. Examples: clubs, halls, parks, museums, and private homes

OPTIONS CONT'D

- The advantage of the first type is that almost everything is done for you. The disadvantage, however, is that your choices of food, china, and linens are limited. Usually you are not permitted to bring in an outside caterer and must select from a predetermined menu

THINGS TO CONSIDER

- The formality of your event
- The site's availability
- Price
- Proximity to the ceremony site
- Ability to accommodate the number of guests in your wedding
- Rental fees for tables, chairs, canopies, etc.
- Food and catering
- Beverages
- Parking
- Gratuity
- Setup fees

- If you are planning an outdoor reception, be sure to have a backup site in case of rain

- Beware: Some hotels are known for double-booking or booking events too close together. Get your rental hours and the name of your room in writing

TIPS TO SAVE MONEY

- You can save money by limiting your guest list; cutting just 10 guests can save over $1,000 many times

- If you hire a wedding consultant, he or she may be able to cut your cake and save you the cake-cutting fee. Check this out with your facility or caterer

- Reception sites that charge a room rental fee may waive this fee if you meet minimum requirements on food and beverages consumed. Try to negotiate this before you book the facility

HORS D'OEUVRES

At receptions where a full meal is to be served, hors d'oeuvres may be offered to guests during the first hour of the reception. However, at a tea or cocktail reception, hors d'oeuvres will serve as the main course.

OPTIONS

- Set hors d'oeuvres out on tables buffet style for guests to help themselves

- Have waiters and waitresses pass hors d'oeuvres on trays

THINGS TO CONSIDER

- Choose foods that can easily be picked up and eaten with one hand, such as skewers or puff pastries
- Avoid serving hors d'oeuvres that are labor intensive or that require expensive ingredients
- Consider whether heating or refrigeration will be available and choose your food accordingly
- When planning your menu, consider the time of day. You should select lighter hors d'oeuvres for a midday reception and heavier hors d'oeuvres for an evening reception
- Compare two or three caterers; there is a wide price range between caterers for the same food

TIPS TO SAVE MONEY

- Pass hors d'oeuvres during cocktail hour and serve a lighter meal
- Consider serving hors d'oeuvres buffet style. Your guests will eat less this way than if waiters and waitresses are constantly serving them

MAIN MEAL & CATERER

If your reception is at a hotel, restaurant or other facility that provides food, you will need to select meals to serve your guests from a predetermined menu. If your venue does not provide food, you will need to hire an outside caterer.

OPTIONS

- Food can be served either buffet style or as a sit-down meal. This should be chosen according to the time of day, year, and formality of the wedding
- Although there are many main dish options, chicken and beef are the most popular selections for a large event
- Ask your facility manager or caterer for their specialty. If you have a special type of food you would like to serve at your reception, select a facility or caterer who specializes in preparing it

THINGS TO CONSIDER

- Your contract should state the amount and type of food and beverages that will be served, the way in which they will be served, the number of servers who will be available, and the cost per food item or person
- Ask for references and look at photos from previous parties so you know how the food will be presented; or better yet, visit an event they are catering

THINGS TO CONSIDER CONT'D

- When hiring a caterer, check to see if the location for your reception provides refrigeration and cooking equipment

- If not, make sure your caterer is fully self-supported with portable refrigeration and heating equipment

- Find out if the caterer will provide a staff of cooks, servers, and bartenders

- If you are unsure about some guests, give only 90 to 95 percent of your final guest count to your caterer or facility manager. If they don't show up, you won't have to pay for extra plates. And if they do, your caterer should still have enough food for all of them (caterers always have a little extra, just in case)

- If offering a buffet meal, have the catering staff serve the food onto guests' plates rather than allowing guests to serve themselves. This will help to regulate the amount of food consumed

- Select food that is not too time-consuming to prepare, or food that does not have expensive ingredients that have to be shipped in from elsewhere

- If having a green wedding, consider the fact that organic menu can raise costs by 10%

- Meat dishes are always more expensive than chicken, fish, or pasta

THINGS TO CONSIDER CONT'D

- Avoid mayonnaise, cream sauces, or custard fillings if food must go unrefrigerated for any length of time

TIPS TO SAVE MONEY

- Consider a brunch or early afternoon wedding. Guests will eat and drink less during the day than at night

LIQUOR/BEVERAGES

Prices for liquor and beverages vary greatly, depending on the amount and brand of alcohol served. Traditionally, at least champagne or punch should be served to toast the couple.

OPTIONS

- Full open bar, where you pay for your guests to drink as much as they wish
- Open bar for the first hour, followed by a cash bar where guests pay for their own drinks
- Cash bar only
- Beer and wine only
- Toasting champagne only
- Nonalcoholic beverages only

THINGS TO CONSIDER

- White and red wines, scotch, vodka, gin, rum, and beer are the most popular alcoholic beverages
- Sodas and fruit punch are popular nonalcoholic beverages served at receptions
- If you serve coffee or tea, ask if your facility charges extra to pour it
- If you plan to serve alcoholic beverages at a reception site that does not provide liquor, make sure your caterer has a license to serve alcohol and that your reception site allows alcoholic beverages
- Ask the catering manager how they charge for liquor: by consumption or by number of bottles opened. Get this in writing before the event and then ask for a full consumption report after the event
- Some reception sites and caterers charge an extra fee for bartending and for setting up the bar
- Check with your caterer about gratuity, which is generally 15 percent to 20 percent of your food and beverage bill
- You may wish to provide your own alcohol; for one, it is more cost effective, and second, you may want to serve an exotic wine or champagne that the reception site or caterer does not offer

THINGS TO CONSIDER CONT'D

- If you buy your own alcohol, be prepared to pay a corkage fee per each bottle brought into the reception site
- Consider whether the expenses saved after paying the corkage fee justify the hassle and liability of bringing in your own alcohol
- If you do order your own alcohol, do so three or four weeks before the event
- For a no-host or cash bar, notify guests so they know to bring cash with them. A simple line that says "No-Host Bar" on the reception card should suffice
- Never serve liquor without some type of food
- For the toast, have waiters pass out champagne only to those guests who want it. Many people will make a toast with whatever they are currently drinking
- On the average, you should plan for one drink per person, per hour at the reception. A bottle of champagne will usually serve six glasses

Use the following chart to determine your beverage needs:

BEVERAGE CHART

- ❑ Bourbon — 3 Fifths
- ❑ Gin — 3 Fifths
- ❑ Rum — 2 Fifths
- ❑ Scotch — 4 Quarts
- ❑ Vodka — 5 Quarts
- ❑ White Wine — 2 Cases
- ❑ Red Wine — 1 Case
- ❑ Champagne — 3 Cases
- ❑ Other — 2 Cases each:
(Club Soda, Seltzer Water, Tonic Water, Ginger Ale, Cola, Beer)

REMEMBER!

- It is not uncommon for the hosts of a party to be held legally responsible for the conduct and safety of their guests. Keep this in mind when planning the quantity and type of beverages to serve. Also, be sure to remind your bartenders not to serve alcohol to minors

TIPS TO SAVE MONEY

- If your caterer allows it, consider buying liquor from a wholesaler who will let you return unopened bottles

- Omit waiters. People tend to drink almost twice as much if there is someone repeatedly asking them if they would like another drink and then bringing drinks to them

TIPS TO SAVE MONEY CONT'D

- Host alcoholic beverages for the first hour, then go to a cash bar. Or host beer, wine, and soft drinks only and have mixed drinks available on a cash basis

SERVICE PROVIDERS' MEALS

You should plan to feed your photographer, videographer, and any other service providers at the reception.

OPTIONS

- Check options and discuss prices for service provider meals with your caterer or reception site manager
- There should be enough food left after all your guests have been served for your service providers to eat. Tell them they are welcome to eat after all your guests have been served
- Make sure you allocate a place for your service providers to eat. You may want them to eat with your guests, or you may prefer setting a place outside the main room for them to eat. Your service providers may be more comfortable with the latter

REMEMBER!

- You don't need to feed your service providers the same meal as your guests. You can order sandwiches or another less expensive meal for them

DECORATIONS

Decorations can range anywhere from floral arrangements, twinkling lights, and centerpieces to more personal touches such as seating cards, menus, favors, and more.

OPTIONS

- Floral arrangements
- Floating candles in vases
- An arrangement of shells for a seaside reception
- A wreath of greenery woven with colored ribbon
- Votive candles set on top of a mirror make a romantic centerpiece for an evening reception

THINGS TO CONSIDER

- Select a table centerpiece that complements your colors and setting

- The centerpiece for the head table should be larger or more elaborate than the ones for the other tables

- Make sure that your centerpiece is kept low enough so as not to hinder conversation among guests seated across from each other

- Consider using a centerpiece that your guests can take home as a memento of your wedding

TIPS TO SAVE MONEY

- Make your own centerpieces using materials that are inexpensive like mason jars, candles, stones, fruit, shells, and succulents. Non-floral items will always make for a less-expensive option

- Transport floral arrangements from the ceremony site at your reception and reuse them.

PARTY FAVORS

Party favors are small gift items given to your guests as mementos of your wedding. They add a very special touch to your wedding and can become keepsakes for your guests.

OPTIONS

- Anything monogrammed or engraved with the couple's names and wedding date

- Individually wrapped and marked nuts or fine candy

- Wine or champagne bottles marked with the bride and groom's names and wedding date on a personalized label

- Handmade edible favors, such as jars of jam or cookies, with the recipe included

- For environmentally conscientious couples, present each guest with a tiny shoot of a tree to be planted in honor of the bride and groom

OPTIONS CONT'D

- For environmentally conscientious couples, present each guest with a tiny shoot of a tree to be planted in honor of the bride and groom

THINGS TO CONSIDER

- Personalized favors need to be ordered several weeks in advance
- Inevitably, favors will get left behind by some guests; guests are most likely to keep their favors if there are of the edible variety
- Try giving away flowers or table centerpieces to guests as favors

Inevitably, favors will get left behind by some guests; guests are most likely to keep their favors if there are of the edible variety

Try giving away flowers or table centerpieces to guests as favors

BRIDE & GROOM SENDOFF

It is tradition that the bride and groom are seen off by their guests as they leave the ceremony and the reception. This tradition was initiated in the Middle Ages whereby a handful of wheat was thrown over the bridal couple as a symbol of fertility.

OPTIONS

- Rose petals
- Rice
- Confetti
- Sparklers
- Grass or flower seeds for an eco-friendly sendoff

THINGS TO CONSIDER

- Ask your reception site about their policy. Many venues will not allow certain things to be tossed, especially those requiring cleanup

- Hand petals or sparklers out to guests wrapped in sachets or packages printed with the couple's names and wedding date

- Be sure to have something on hand to light guests' sparklers

- Consider that rose petals can stain carpets; rice can sting faces, harm birds and make stairs dangerously slippery; and confetti is messy and hard to clean up

GIFT ATTENDANT

The gift attendant is responsible for watching over your gifts during the reception.

THINGS TO CONSIDER

- A gift attendant is only necessary if your reception is held in a public area such as a hotel or outside garden where strangers may be walking by
- Do not ask a friend or family member take on this duty as he or she will want enjoy the reception
- Hire a young boy or girl from your neighborhood
- The gift attendant should also be responsible for transporting your gifts from the reception site to your car or bridal suite

PARKING FEE & VALET SERVICES

Depending on where you host your wedding reception, there may be a need for paid parking or valet service.

THINGS TO CONSIDER

- Many hotels, restaurants, etc. charge for parking. It is customary, although not necessary, for the host of the wedding to pay this charge
- For a home reception, hire a valet service if parking is limited
- Consider having guests park in a church or school lot nearby and hire a van to take them to the reception site

THINGS TO CONSIDER CONT'D

- Always make sure a valet service is fully insured

- When comparing the cost of reception sites, don't forget to add the cost of parking to the total price

NOTES

QUESTIONS TO ASK ABOUT RECEPTION SITES

Use these questions to compare and contrast different reception locations you are considering.

BE SURE TO ASK

- What is the name of the reception site?

Option 1 ....

Option 2 ....

- What is your website?

Option 1 ....

Option 2 ....

- What is your e-mail?

Option 1 ....

Option 2 ....

- What is your address?

Option 1 ....

Option 2 ....

- What is the name of my contact person?

Option 1 ....

Option 2 ....

- What is his or her phone number?

Option 1 ....

Option 2 ....

BE SURE TO ASK CONT'D

- What dates and times are available?

Option 1 ....

Option 2 ....

- What is the maximum number of guests for a seated reception?

Option 1 ....

Option 2 ....

- What is the maximum number of guests for a cocktail reception?

Option 1 ....

Option 2 ....

- What is the reception site fee?

Option 1 ....

Option 2 ....

- What is the price range for a seated lunch?

Option 1 ....

Option 2 ....

- What is the price range for a buffet lunch?

Option 1 ....

Option 2 ....

BE SURE TO ASK CONT'D

- What is the price range for a seated dinner?

Option 1 ....

Option 2 ....

- What is the price range for a buffet dinner?

Option 1 ....

Option 2 ....

- What is the corkage fee?

Option 1 ....

Option 2 ....

- What is the cake-cutting fee?

Option 1 ....

Option 2 ....

- What is the ratio of servers to guests?

Option 1 ....

Option 2 ....

- How much time will be allotted for my reception?

Option 1 ....

Option 2 ....

- What music restrictions are there, if any?

Option 1 ....

Option 2 ....

BE SURE TO ASK CONT'D

✼ What alcohol restrictions are there, if any?

Option 1 ....

Option 2 ....

✼ Are there any restrictions for rice/rose petal tossing?

Option 1 ....

Option 2 ....

✼ What room and table decorations are available?

Option 1 ....

Option 2 ....

✼ Is a changing room available?

Option 1 ....

Option 2 ....

✼ Is there handicap accessibility?

Option 1 ....

Option 2 ....

✼ Is a dance floor included in the site fee?

Option 1 ....

Option 2 ....

✼ Are tables, chairs, and linens included in the site fee?

Option 1 ....

Option 2 ....

BE SURE TO ASK CONT'D

- Are outside caterers allowed?

Option 1 ....

Option 2 ....

- Are kitchen facilities available for outside caterers?

Option 1 ....

Option 2 ....

- Does the facility have full liability insurance?

Option 1 ....

Option 2 ....

- What perks or giveaways are offered?

Option 1 ....

Option 2 ....

- How much parking is available for my bridal party?

Option 1 ....

Option 2 ....

- How much parking is available for my guests?

Option 1 ....

Option 2 ....

- What is the cost for parking, if any?

Option 1 ....

Option 2 ....

BE SURE TO ASK CONT'D

- What is the cost for sleeping rooms, if available?

Option 1 ....

Option 2 ....

- What is the payment policy?

Option 1 ....

Option 2 ....

- What is the cancellation policy?

Option 1 ....

Option 2 ....

- Other ....

Option 1 ....

Option 2 ....

- Other ....

Option 1 ....

Option 2 ....

- Other ....

Option 1 ....

Option 2 ....

- Other ....

Option 1 ....

Option 2 ....

RECEPTION SITE INFORMATION

Use this form to organize the information about your final reception site selection.

RECEPTION SITE AT-A-GLANCE

Location: ....

Site Coordinator: ....

Website: ....

E-mail: ....

Phone: .... Fax: ....

Address: ....

City/State/Zip Code: ....

Name of Room: ....

Room Capacity: ....

Date Confirmed: ....

Confirm Head Count By: ....

Beginning Time: ....

Ending Time: ....

Cocktails/Hors d'Oeuvres Time: ....

Meal Time: ....

Color of Linens/Napkins: ....

RECEPTION SITE AT-A-GLANCE CONT'D

Total Cost: ....

Deposit: ....Date: ....

Balance: .... Date Due: ....

Cancellation Policy: ....

Notes: ....

....

....

....

....

EQUIPMENT INCLUDES

- ❑ Tables
- ❑ Chairs
- ❑ Linens
- ❑ Tableware
- ❑ Barware
- ❑ Heaters
- ❑ Electric Outlet
- ❑ Musical Instruments

SERVICE INCLUDES

- ❑ Waiters
- ❑ Bartenders
- ❑ Valet
- ❑ Main Meal
- ❑ Clean Up
- ❑ Setup
- ❑ Security
- ❑ Free Parking

QUESTIONS TO ASK CATERERS

Use these questions to compare and contrast different caterers you are considering.

▶ BE SURE TO ASK

- What is the name of your company?

Option 1 ....

Option 2 ....

- What is your website?

Option 1 ....

Option 2 ....

- What is your e-mail?

Option 1 ....

Option 2 ....

- What is your address?

Option 1 ....

Option 2 ....

- What is the name of my contact person?

Option 1 ....

Option 2 ....

- What is his or her phone number?

Option 1 ....

Option 2 ....

BE SURE TO ASK CONT'D

- How many years have you been in business?

Option 1 ....

Option 2 ....

- What percentage of your business is dedicated to receptions?

Option 1 ....

Option 2 ....

- Do you have liability insurance and a license to serve alcohol?

Option 1 ....

Option 2 ....

- When is the final head-count needed?

Option 1 ....

Option 2 ....

- What is your ratio of servers to guests?

Option 1 ....

Option 2 ....

- How do your servers dress for wedding receptions?

Option 1 ....

Option 2 ....

BE SURE TO ASK CONT'D

- What is your price range for a seated lunch/buffet lunch?

Option 1 ....

Option 2 ....

- What is your price range for a seated dinner/buffet dinner?

Option 1 ....

Option 2 ....

- How much gratuity is expected?

Option 1 ....

Option 2 ....

- What is your specialty?

Option 1 ....

Option 2 ....

- What is your cake-cutting fee?

Option 1 ....

Option 2 ....

- What is your bartending fee?

Option 1 ....

Option 2 ....

BE SURE TO ASK CONT'D

✼ What is your fee to clean up after the reception?

Option 1 ....

Option 2 ....

✼ What is your payment policy?

Option 1 ....

Option 2 ....

✼ What is your cancellation policy?

Option 1 ....

Option 2 ....

✼ Other ....

Option 1 ....

Option 2 ....

✼ Other ....

Option 1 ....

Option 2 ....

✼ Other ....

Option 1 ....

Option 2 ....

✼ Other ....

Option 1 ....

Option 2 ....

CATERER INFORMATION

Use this form to organize the information about your final caterer selection.

CATERER AT-A-GLANCE

Contact Person:

Cost Per Person:

Website:

E-mail:

Phone:

Fax:

Address:

City/ State/Zip Code:

Confirmed Date:

Confirm Head Count By:

Arrival Time:

Departure Time:

Cocktails/Hors d'Oeuvres Time:

Meal Time:

Color of Linens:

Color of Napkins:

CATERER AT-A-GLANCE CONT'D

Total Cost: ....

Deposit: .... Date: ....

Balance: .... Date Due: ....

Cancellation Policy: ....

Notes: ....

....

....

....

....

EQUIPMENT INCLUDES

❑ Tables	❑ Linens	❑ Barware	❑ Lighting
❑ Chairs	❑ Tableware	❑ Heaters	❑ Candles

SERVICE INCLUDES

❑ Waiters	❑ Hors d'Oeuvres	❑ Wine/Beer
❑ Bartenders	❑ Buffet Meal	❑ Punch
❑ Setup	❑ Seated Meal	❑ Soft Drinks
❑ Clean Up	❑ Cocktails	❑ Coffee/Tea
❑ Security	❑ Champagne	❑ Cake

MENU WORKSHEET

HORS D'OEUVRES:

....

....

....

....

....

SALADS/APPETIZERS:

....

....

....

....

....

SOUPS:

....

....

....

....

....

MENU WORKSHEET CONT'D

MAIN ENTREE:

....

....

....

....

....

DESSERTS:

....

....

....

....

....

WEDDING CAKE:

....

....

....

....

....

LIQUOR ORDER FORM

Liquor Store: ....

Date Ordered: ....

Salesperson: ....

Phone Number: ....

Website: ....

E-mail: ....

Address: ....

City/State/Zip Code: ....

Cost: ....

Delivered By: ....

Delivery Date: ....

Type of Liquor:	# of Bottles Needed:	Price:

PARTY FAVORS COMPARISON SHEET

Use this form to organize the information about your final party favor selections.

PARTY FAVOR SELECTIONS

- **Type of Favor:** ....

Website/Company: ....

Quantity: .... Price: ....

- **Type of Favor:** ....

Website/Company: ....

Quantity: .... Price: ....

- **Type of Favor:** ....

Website/Company: ....

Quantity: .... Price: ....

- **Type of Favor:** ....

Website/Company: ....

Quantity: .... Price: ....

- **Type of Favor:** ....

Website/Company: ....

Quantity: .... Price: ....

THINGS TO DO

- [ ]
- [ ]
- [ ]
- [ ]
- [ ]

NOTES

Music

You want your wedding to be beautiful and memorable. Music plays a big part in making that happen. It will serve as the soundtrack to your day and will help convey the feelings you have for each other and for your families and friends.

CEREMONY MUSIC

Ceremony music is the music played during the prelude, processional, ceremony, recessional, and postlude.

OPTIONS

- Organ
- Piano
- Harp
- Guitar
- Flutes

POPULAR SELECTIONS: CHRISTIAN

- Trumpet Voluntary by Purcell
- The Bridal Chorus by Wagner
- Wedding March by Mendelssohn

POPULAR SELECTIONS: CHRISTIAN CONT'D

- Postlude in G Major by Handel
- Canon in D Major by Pachelbel
- Adagio in A Minor by Bach

POPULAR SELECTIONS: JEWISH

- Erev Shel Shoshanim
- Erev Ba
- Hana' Ava Babanot

THINGS TO CONSIDER

- When selecting ceremony music, keep in mind the formality of your wedding, your religious affiliation, and the length of the ceremony

- If your ceremony is outside, there may be other noises such as traffic, wind, or people's voices, so consider having the music, your officiant, and your vows amplified

- Ask if music is included as part of your ceremony site fee

- Check with your ceremony site about restrictions pertaining to music and the availability of musical instruments for your use

- Make sure there are electrical outlets close to where the instruments will be set up

THINGS TO CONSIDER CONT'D

- Discuss the selection of ceremony music with your officiant and musicians
- Make sure the musicians know how to play the selections you request
- If you hire a band for your reception, consider having a scaled-down version of the same group play at your ceremony, such as a trio of flute, guitar, and vocals. This might also enable you to negotiate a package price
- Have a DJ play pre-recorded music at your ceremony

TIPS TO SAVE MONEY

- Hire student musicians from your local university or high school to play
- Consider asking a friend to sing or play at your ceremony; he or she will be honored

SECTIONS OF THE CEREMONY

Select appropriate music for the following times before, during and after the ceremony.

CEREMONY MUSIC

Prelude

- Period of time before the ceremony begins
- Guests will be arriving and taking their seats

Pre-Processional

- The time just before the procession of the wedding party begins
- Important family members, such as the mother-of-the-bride, are ushered to their seats
- Lets your guests know that the ceremony is about to begin
- A way to honor family members who are especially important to you

Processional

- Plays as the bridal party walks down the aisle
- The music should switch from pre-processional to processional when the wedding party appears at the top of the aisle
- Should have a tempo that allows the wedding party to walk down the aisle at a measured pace

Bride's Processional

- Plays as soon as the bride appears at the top of the aisle

CEREMONY MUSIC CONT'D

Ceremony

- Have favorite songs playing softly as background music throughout the ceremony
- Take a break in the ceremony to have a favorite hymn sung in place of a reading
- Set the lighting of your unity candle to music
- Opt to have no music at all

Recessional

- Begins as soon as you are pronounced husband and wife
- Plays while you and your new spouse will walk back up the aisle

Postlude

- The time between the end of the ceremony and the beginning of the reception
- Use this time to take wedding party pictures or to greet guests in a receiving line
- Should be non-intrusive to allow for conversation while your guests mingle and enjoy refreshments and hors d'oeuvres

CEREMONY MUSIC SELECTIONS

Use this form to organize your ceremony music selections.

CEREMONY MUSIC

- Part of Ceremony:

  Song/Selection:

  Artist/Composer:

  Played by:

- Part of Ceremony:

  Song/Selection:

  Artist/Composer:

  Played by:

- Part of Ceremony:

  Song/Selection:

  Artist/Composer:

  Played by:

- Part of Ceremony:

  Song/Selection:

  Artist/Composer:

  Played by:

- Part of Ceremony:

  Song/Selection:

  Artist/Composer:

  Played by:

- Part of Ceremony:

  Song/Selection:

  Artist/Composer:

  Played by:

- Part of Ceremony:

  Song/Selection:

  Artist/Composer:

  Played by:

- Part of Ceremony:

  Song/Selection:

  Artist/Composer:

  Played by:

- Part of Ceremony:

  Song/Selection:

  Artist/Composer:

  Played by:

QUESTIONS TO ASK CEREMONY MUSICIANS

Use these questions to compare and contrast different ceremony musicians you are considering.

BE SURE TO ASK

- What is the name of your company?

Option 1 ....

Option 2 ....

- What is your website?

Option 1 ....

Option 2 ....

- What is your e-mail?

Option 1 ....

Option 2 ....

- What is your address?

Option 1 ....

Option 2 ....

- What is the name of my contact person?

Option 1 ....

Option 2 ....

- What is his or her phone number?

Option 1 ....

Option 2 ....

BE SURE TO ASK CONT'D

- How many years have you been in business?

Option 1 ....

Option 2 ....

- What percentage of your business is dedicated to weddings?

Option 1 ....

Option 2 ....

- Are you the person who will perform at my wedding?

Option 1 ....

Option 2 ....

- What instrument(s) do you play?

Option 1 ....

Option 2 ....

- What type of music do you specialize in?

Option 1 ....

Option 2 ....

- What are your hourly fees?

Option 1 ....

Option 2 ....

BE SURE TO ASK CONT'D

- What is the cost of a soloist?

Option 1 ....

Option 2 ....

- What is the cost of a duet?

Option 1 ....

Option 2 ....

- What is the cost of a trio?

Option 1 ....

Option 2 ....

- What is the cost of a quartet?

Option 1 ....

Option 2 ....

- How would you dress for my wedding?

Option 1 ....

Option 2 ....

- Do you have liability insurance?

Option 1 ....

Option 2 ....

- Do you have a cordless microphone?

Option 1 ....

Option 2 ....

BE SURE TO ASK CONT'D

- What is your payment policy?

Option 1 ....

Option 2 ....

- What is your cancellation policy?

Option 1 ....

Option 2 ....

- Other ....

Option 1 ....

Option 2 ....

- Other ....

Option 1 ....

Option 2 ....

- Other ....

Option 1 ....

Option 2 ....

- Other ....

Option 1 ....

Option 2 ....

- Other ....

Option 1 ....

Option 2 ....

CEREMONY MUSIC INFORMATION

Use this form to organize the information about your final ceremony musician selection.

CEREMONY MUSIC AT-A-GLANCE

- Company Name:
- Contact Person:
- Website:
- Email:
- Address:
- City:
- State/Zip Code:
- Phone Number:
- Payment Policy:
- Cancellation Policy:
- Notes:

RECEPTION MUSIC

Music is a major part of your reception, and should be planned carefully. Music helps create the atmosphere of your wedding. Special songs will make your reception unique.

OPTIONS

- DJ
- Band
- Orchestra
- Combination of one or more instruments and vocalists

THINGS TO CONSIDER

- Keep in mind the age and musical preference of your guests
- Bands and live musicians are typically more expensive than DJs
- A professional DJ will be able to play a wider variety of music than live musicians
- Does your venue have any restrictions on music?
- Hire an entertainment agency that can help you choose a reliable DJ or band
- Hire someone with experience performing at wedding receptions

THINGS TO CONSIDER CONT'D

- Consider watching your musicians perform at a similar event before booking their services
- Give your DJ a complete timeline for your reception in order to announce the various events such as the toasts, first dance, and cutting of the cake
- Make a list of songs you want played and the sequence in which you want them played and give it to your DJ
- Make sure there are electrical outlets close to where musicians will be performing
- Create songs playlists for the cocktail hour (15 to 20 medium-tempo songs), dinner (35 mellow melodies), and post-dinner (50 or more fast-dance songs, plus a few slow songs)

TIPS TO SAVE MONEY

- Some facilities have contracts with certain DJs, and you may be able to save money by hiring one of them
- Check the music department of local colleges and universities for names of student musicians and DJs

RECEPTION MUSIC SELECTIONS

Choose the music for the following portions of your reception and give it to your DJ or musicians.

RECEPTION MUSIC

- **Receiving Line**

  Song/Selection: ....

  Artist/Composer: ....

- **During Hors d'Oeuvres**

  Song/Selection: ....

  Artist/Composer: ....

- **During Dinner**

  Song/Selection: ....

  Artist/Composer: ....

- **First Dance**

  Song/Selection: ....

  Artist/Composer: ....

- **Second Dance**

  Song/Selection: ....

  Artist/Composer: ....

- **Third Dance**

  Song/Selection: ....

  Artist/Composer: ....

RECEPTION MUSIC CONT'D

Bouquet Toss

Song/Selection:

Artist/Composer:

Garter Removal

Song/Selection:

Artist/Composer:

Cutting of the Cake

Song/Selection:

Artist/Composer:

Last Dance

Song/Selection:

Artist/Composer:

Couple Leaving

Song/Selection:

Artist/Composer:

Other:

Song/Selection:

Artist/Composer:

Other:

Song/Selection:

Artist/Composer:

RECEPTION MUSIC CONT'D

- **Other:** ....

  Song/Selection: ....

  Artist/Composer: ....
- **Other:** ....

  Song/Selection: ....

  Artist/Composer: ....
- **Other:** ....

  Song/Selection: ....

  Artist/Composer: ....
- **Other:** ....

  Song/Selection: ....

  Artist/Composer: ....
- **Other:** ....

  Song/Selection: ....

  Artist/Composer: ....
- **Other:** ....

  Song/Selection: ....

  Artist/Composer: ....
- **Other:** ....

  Song/Selection: ....

  Artist/Composer: ....

QUESTIONS TO ASK RECEPTION MUSICIANS

Use these questions to compare and contrast different reception musicians/DJs you are considering.

BE SURE TO ASK

- What is the name of your company?

Option 1 ....

Option 2 ....

- What is your website?

Option 1 ....

Option 2 ....

- What is your e-mail?

Option 1 ....

Option 2 ....

- What is your address?

Option 1 ....

Option 2 ....

- What is the name of my contact person?

Option 1 ....

Option 2 ....

- What is his or her phone number?

Option 1 ....

Option 2 ....

BE SURE TO ASK CONT'D

* How many years have you been in business?

Option 1 ....

Option 2 ....

* What percentage of your business is dedicated to weddings?

Option 1 ....

Option 2 ....

* How many people are in your band?

Option 1 ....

Option 2 ....

* What type of music do you specialize in?

Option 1 ....

Option 2 ....

* What type of sound system do you have?

Option 1 ....

Option 2 ....

* Can you act as a master of ceremonies? How do you dress?

Option 1 ....

Option 2 ....

BE SURE TO ASK CONT'D

- How will you dress at my reception?

Option 1 ....

Option 2 ....

- Do you have a cordless microphone?

Option 1 ....

Option 2 ....

- How many breaks do you take? How long are they?

Option 1 ....

Option 2 ....

- Do you play recorded music during breaks?

Option 1 ....

Option 2 ....

- Do you have liability insurance?

Option 1 ....

Option 2 ....

- What are your fees for a 4-hour reception?

Option 1 ....

Option 2 ....

- What is your cost for each additional hour?

Option 1 ....

Option 2 ....

RECEPTION MUSIC INFORMATION

Use this form to organize the information about your final ceremony musician selection.

RECEPTION MUSIC AT-A-GLANCE

- Company Name:
- Contact Person:
- Website:
- Email:
- Address:
- City:
- State/Zip Code:
- Phone Number:
- Payment Policy:
- Cancellation Policy:
- Notes:

THINGS TO DO

- ❑
- ❑
- ❑
- ❑
- ❑

NOTES

Bakery

Wedding cakes may be ordered from a caterer or from a bakery. Some hotels and restaurants may also be able to provide a wedding cake. However, you will probably be better off ordering your cake from a bakery that specializes in wedding cakes.

WEDDING CAKE

When ordering your wedding cake, you will have to decide not only on a flavor, but also on a size, shape, and color.

OPTIONS

- Order from a caterer or from a bakery that specializes in wedding cakes
- Some hotels and restaurants may also be able to provide a wedding cake
- Choose one large tier or several smaller tiers
- Choose round, square, or heart-shaped

OPTIONS CONT'D

- The most common flavors are chocolate, carrot, lemon, rum, and "white" cake
- Be creative by adding a filling to your cake, such as custard, mousse, fruit, or chocolate
- Consider having tiers of different flavors if you and your partner can't agree

THINGS TO CONSIDER

- Size of the cake is determined by the number of guests
- Don't forget that you'll be saving the top tier for your first anniversary. This top tier should be removed before the cake is cut, wrapped in several layers of plastic wrap or put inside a plastic container, and kept frozen until your anniversary
- Price, workmanship, quality, and taste vary considerably from baker to baker. Ask to see photographs of other wedding cakes your baker has created
- Consider decoration and spoilage (sugar keeps longer than cream frostings)
- Arrange to have a beautiful cake-cutting knife from your baker, caterer, or reception site manager, or purchase your own

THINGS TO CONSIDER CONT'D

- Schedule cake tastings
- Most reception sites and caterers charge a fee for each slice of cake they cut if the cake is brought in from an outside bakery
- Check to see if your baker has setup and delivery fees
- Check to see if your caterer has contracts with bakeries
- Consider whether you have specific needs, such as food allergies or kosher ingredients, and find a baker who will work with those requests
- Talk to your baker about how much cake to order. You may only need to order cake for 75 percent of your RSVP list, for instance

TIPS TO SAVE MONEY

- Some bakeries require a deposit on columns and plates; other bakeries use disposable columns and plates, saving you the rental fee and the hassle of returning these items
- Have a friend or family member get a quick lesson on how to set up your cake to save on setup fees; have him or her pick it up and set it up the day of your wedding

TIPS TO SAVE MONEY CONT'D

- Flowers make beautiful cake decorations and cost less than some edible decorations like fondant

- Many hotels and restaurants include a dessert in the cost of their meal packages. If you forego this dessert and substitute your cake as the dessert, they may be willing to waive the cake-cutting fee

- Some couples will purchase one high-end cake to display and cut during the reception and serve regular sheet cake to guests from the kitchen. No one is ever the wiser!

UNIQUE ALTERNATIVES

- Cupcakes are a growing trend that can save money

- Individual cakes, tarts, or fruit pies are a nice alternative to a cake for a smaller wedding

- If you have friends and family who bake, consider asking them for help creating your cake alternative. A dessert bar filled with fudge, cupcakes, cookies, and other desserts is a nice option

CAKE TOP

The bride's cake is often topped with fresh flowers or traditional cake tops (figurines set atop the wedding cake).

OPTIONS

- A figurine of a bridal couple
- Replica of two wedding rings
- Fresh flowers
- Monogram of the couple's initials
- Bells
- Love birds

TIPS TO SAVE MONEY

- Borrow a cake top from a friend or a family member as your "something borrowed"

REMEMBER!

- Some porcelain and heavier cake toppers need to be anchored down into the cake. Be sure to discuss this with your baker

CAKE KNIFE/TOASTING GLASSES

The cake knife is used to cut the cake at the reception. The bride usually cuts the first two slices of the wedding cake with the groom's hand placed over hers. The groom feeds the bride first. Then the bride feeds the groom.

You will need toasting glasses to toast each other after cutting the cake. They are usually decorated with ribbons or flowers and kept near the cake.

THINGS TO CONSIDER

- Have your initials and wedding date engraved on your wedding knife as a memento
- Consider purchasing crystal or silver toasting glasses as a keepsake of your wedding
- Have your florist decorate your knife and toasting glasses with flowers or ribbons

TIPS TO SAVE MONEY

- Borrow your cake knife or toasting glasses from a friend or family member as "something borrowed"
- Use the reception facility's glasses and knife, and decorate them with flowers or ribbon

CAKE DISPLAY TABLE

Your cake should be displayed for guests to see. Talk to your event designer or florist about making this area attractive.

THINGS TO CONSIDER

- Purchase, rent, or borrow a pretty cake stand
- Have your florist or event designer decorate the table around the cake
- Consider decorating the table with personal photos, including your engagement or bridal portraits
- Have your bridesmaids place their bouquets on the cake table during the reception
- Leave decorations to your florist, who will know to use only nonpoisonous flowers

GROOM'S CAKE

The groom's cake is an old Southern tradition whereby a small additional cake is cut up and sent home with guests in little white boxes engraved with the bride and groom's names. Modernly, the groom's cake, if offered, is cut and served along with the wedding cake.

OPTIONS

- Traditionally, the groom's cake is a chocolate cake decorated with fruit

THINGS TO CONSIDER

- Consider a theme relating to the groom, i.e., favorite sport, team, hobby, etc.
- To save money, you may want to skip this custom

NOTES

QUESTIONS TO ASK THE BAKERY

Use these questions to compare and contrast different bakers you are considering.

BE SURE TO ASK

- What is the name of your company?

Option 1 ....

Option 2 ....

- What is your website?

Option 1 ....

Option 2 ....

- What is your e-mail?

Option 1 ....

Option 2 ....

- What is your address?

Option 1 ....

Option 2 ....

- What is the name of my contact person?

Option 1 ....

Option 2 ....

- What is his or her phone number?

Option 1 ....

Option 2 ....

BE SURE TO ASK CONT'D

- How long have you been making wedding cakes?

Option 1 ....

Option 2 ....

- What are your wedding cake specialties?

Option 1 ....

Option 2 ....

- Do you offer free tastings of your wedding cakes?

Option 1 ....

Option 2 ....

- Are your wedding cakes fresh or frozen?

Option 1 ....

Option 2 ....

- How far in advance should I order my cake?

Option 1 ....

Option 2 ....

- Can you make a groom's cake?

Option 1 ....

Option 2 ....

- Do you lend, rent, or sell cake knives?

Option 1 ....

Option 2 ....

BE SURE TO ASK CONT'D

❊ What is the cost per serving of my desired cake?

Option 1 ....

Option 2 ....

❊ What is your cake pillar and plate rental fee, if any?

Option 1 ....

Option 2 ....

❊ Is this fee refundable upon the return of these items?

Option 1 ....

Option 2 ....

❊ When must these items be returned?

Option 1 ....

Option 2 ....

❊ What is your cake delivery and setup fee?

Option 1 ....

Option 2 ....

❊ What is your payment policy?

Option 1 ....

Option 2 ....

❊ What is your cancellation policy?

Option 1 ....

Option 2 ....

BAKER INFORMATION

Use this form to organize the information about your final wedding cake and baker selection.

BAKER AT-A-GLANCE

- Company Name:..
- Contact Person:..
- Website:..
- Email:..
- Address:..
- City:..
- State/Zip Code:..
- Phone Number:..
- Payment Policy: ....
- Cancellation Policy:..
- Wedding Cake Details: ....

  ....

  ....

  ....
- Groom's Cake Details..

  ....

Flowers

Flowers add beauty, fragrance, and color to your wedding. The floral choices you make will create an ambience and style, from rustic to elegant to casual to dramatic.

FLOWERS

Like all other aspects of your wedding, flowers should fit your style, theme, season, and color scheme.

THINGS TO CONSIDER

- Select flowers that are in season to assure availability
- Final arrangements should be made well in advance of your wedding date to ensure availability
- Confirm your final order and delivery time a few days before the wedding

THINGS TO CONSIDER CONT'D

- Make sure your florist knows where your sites are and what time to arrive for setup
- Most florists charge a fee to deliver flowers and to arrange them on site
- Avoid scheduling your wedding near holidays such as Valentine's Day and Mother's Day as the price of flowers will be higher

BRIDE'S BOUQUET

The bridal bouquet is one of the most important elements of the bride's attire and deserves special attention to the flower types, colors, and shape.

OPTIONS

- Popular styles are the cascade, cluster, contemporary, and hand-tied garden bouquets
- The traditional bridal bouquet is made of white flowers. Stephanotis, gardenias, white roses, orchids, and lilies of the valley are popular choices for an all-white bouquet
- If you prefer a colorful bouquet, you may want to consider using roses, tulips, stock, peonies, freesia, and gerbera, which come in a wide variety of colors

OPTIONS CONT'D

- Popular fragrant flowers are gardenias, freesia, stephanotis, bouvardia, and narcissus

THINGS TO CONSIDER

- Your flowers should complement the season, gown, color scheme, your attendants' attire, and the style and formality of your wedding
- If you have a favorite flower, build your bouquet around it and include it in all your arrangements
- Some flowers carry centuries of symbolism. Consider stephanotis for good luck, pimpernel for change, forget-me-nots to indicate true love, and ivy for friendship, fidelity, and matrimony
- Orange blossom has at least 700 years of nuptial history; its unusual ability to simultaneously bear flowers and produce fruit symbolizes the fusion of beauty, personality, and fertility
- Have the bouquets delivered before the photographer arrives so that you can include them in your pre-ceremony photos
- In determining the size of your bouquet, consider your gown and your overall stature. Carry a smaller bouquet if you're petite or if your gown is fairly ornate. A long, cascading bouquet complements a fairly simple gown or a tall or larger bride

THINGS TO CONSIDER CONT'D

- For a natural, fresh-picked look, have your florist put together a cluster of flowers tied together with a ribbon
- For a Victorian appeal, carry a nosegay or a basket filled with flowers. Or carry a Bible or other family heirloom decorated with just a few flowers
- For a contemporary look, you may want to consider carrying an arrangement of calla lilies or other long-stemmed flowers over your arm
- For a dramatic statement, carry a single stem of your favorite flower
- If you want to preserve your bridal bouquet, consider having your florist make a smaller, less expensive bouquet specifically for the bouquet toss
- Ask your florist if he or she can design your bridal bouquet in such a way that the center flowers may be removed and worn as a corsage

REMEMBER!

- If your bouquet includes delicate flowers that will not withstand hours of heat or a lack of water, make sure your florist uses a bouquet holder to keep them fresh

TIPS TO SAVE MONEY

- Avoid exotic, out-of-season flowers, which cost significantly more. Try to select flowers that are in bloom and plentiful at the time of your wedding
- Allow your florist to emphasize your colors using more reasonable, seasonal flowers to achieve your overall look

WEDDING PARTY BOUQUETS

The bridesmaids' bouquets should complement the bridal bouquet, but are generally smaller in size.

OPTIONS

- Bridesmaids' bouquets can be identical
- Or, to personalize your bridesmaids' bouquets, choose a different flower for each of their bouquets. For instance, to tell a friend that you admire her, choose yellow jasmine for her bouquet
- The Maid of Honor's bouquet can be somewhat larger or of a different color than the rest of the bridesmaids' bouquets. This will help to set her apart from the others
- Choose a bouquet style (cascade, cluster, contemporary, hand-tied) that complements the formality of your wedding and the height of your attendants

OPTIONS CONT'D

- For a garden look, have your bridesmaids wear garlands of flowers in their hair

TIPS TO SAVE MONEY

- Have your attendants carry a single stemmed rose, lily, or other suitable flower for an elegant look that also saves money

FLOWER GIRL'S HAIRPIECE

Flower girls often wear floral hairpieces.

OPTIONS

- Have your florist create a wreath of small flowers
- If the flowers used for the hairpiece are not a sturdy and long-lived variety, a ribbon, bow, or hat might be a safer choice
- Artificial flowers may be used

FAMILY MEMBERS' CORSAGES

The groom is responsible for providing flowers for his mother, the bride's mother, and the grandmothers. This is so they feel more included in your wedding and guests will know that they are related to the bride and groom.

OPTIONS

- Order flowers that can be pinned to a pocketbook or worn around a wrist
- The officiant, if female, may also be given a corsage to reflect her important role in the ceremony
- Gardenias, camellias, white orchids, or cymbidium orchids are excellent choices for corsages

THINGS TO CONSIDER

- The groom may also want to consider ordering corsages for other close family members, such as sisters and aunts
- Put a protective shield under lilies when using them as corsages, as their anthers will easily stain fabric
- Be careful when using alstroemeria as corsages, as its sap can be harmful if it enters the human bloodstream

TIPS TO SAVE MONEY

- Ask your florist to recommend reasonably priced flowers for corsages.

GROOM'S BOUTONNIERE

The groom wears this on the left lapel, nearest to his heart.

OPTIONS

- Boutonnieres are generally a single blossom such as a rosebud, stephanotis, freesia, or a miniature carnation
- Use a small cluster of flowers tied or pinned together
- Use a mini-carnation rather than a rose to save money

USHERS' & OTHER FAMILY MEMBERS' BOUTONNIERES

The groom gives each man in his wedding party a boutonniere to wear on his left lapel.

OPTIONS

- Generally, a single blossom such as a rosebud, freesia, or miniature carnation is used as ushers' boutonniere
- The officiant, if male, may also be given a boutonniere to reflect his important role in the ceremony

OPTIONS CONT'D

- The ring bearer may or may not wear a boutonniere, depending on his outfit
- The groom should also consider ordering boutonnieres for other close family member such as fathers, grandfathers, and brothers

MAIN ALTAR

The purpose of flowers at the main altar is to direct the guests' visual attention toward the front of the church or synagogue and to the bridal couple.

OPTIONS

- Decorate the arch, gazebo, or other structure serving as the altar with flowers or greenery
- In a Jewish ceremony, vows are said under a Chuppah, which is placed at the altar and covered with greenery and fresh flowers
- Some churches and synagogues are ornate enough and don't need extra flowers. Select a few showpieces that will complement the existing decor

THINGS TO CONSIDER

- Be sure to ask if there are any restrictions on flowers at the church or synagogue

- Remember, decorations should be determined by the size and style of the building, the formality of the wedding, the preferences of the bride, the cost, and the regulations of the particular site

- Decorate with candlelight and greenery only

- Have your ceremony outside in a beautiful garden or by the water, providing natural decor

TIPS TO SAVE MONEY

- Decorate the ceremony site with greenery to cut costs

- Use greenery and flowers from your own garden

- Have your ceremony florals transported to the reception site after the processional so you can reuse the decorations

- Outdoor lighting can be a simple, beautiful touch that eliminates the need for expensive flowers. Consider hanging strings of inexpensive lights or lanterns with candles throughout your ceremony site

AISLE PEWS

Flowers, candles, or ribbons are often used to mark the aisle pews and add color.

OPTIONS

- A cluster or cascade of flowers or a cascade of greens are all popular choices
- Candles with greenery add an elegant touch
- Cascading ribbons in your wedding colors are a beautiful non-floral alternative

THINGS TO CONSIDER

- Use hardy flowers that can tolerate being handled as pew ornaments. Gardenias and camellias, for example, are too sensitive to last long
- Avoid using allium in your aisle pew decorations as they have an odor of onions

TIPS TO SAVE MONEY

- Decorate only the reserved family pews
- Or, decorate every second or third pew

HEAD TABLE

The head table is where the wedding party will sit during the reception. Flowers on this table denote that this is special table at the reception.

OPTIONS

- A cluster of flowers or a cascade of flowers and ribbons
- Decorate the head table with the attendants' bouquets

THINGS TO CONSIDER

- Consider using a different color or style of arrangement to set the head table apart from the other tables
- Avoid using highly fragrant flowers, such as narcissus, on tables where food is being served or eaten, as their fragrance may conflict with other aromas

TIPS TO SAVE MONEY

- Reuse flowers from the ceremony at the reception site
- Use greenery rather than flowers to fill large areas
- Candles are inexpensive and lend a romantic feel to your reception

GUEST TABLES

At a reception where guests are seated, a small flower arrangement may be placed on each table.

THINGS TO CONSIDER

- The arrangements should complement the table linens and the size of the table
- Flowers should be kept low enough so as not to hinder conversation among guests
- Avoid using highly fragrant flowers, like narcissus, on tables where food is being eaten

TIPS TO SAVE MONEY

- Use small potted flowering plants placed in white baskets or tin pots
- Place a wreath of greenery entwined with colored ribbon in the center of each table
- Give floral arrangements later as gifts to guests

BUFFET TABLES

If buffet tables are used, have some type of floral arrangement to add color and beauty to your display.

OPTIONS

- Put small arrangements of flowers between courses on a buffet table
- Herbs lend a rustic touch. Try a mixture of rosemary and mint combined with scented geraniums

THINGS TO CONSIDER

- Depending on the size of the table, place one or two arrangements at each side
- Avoid placing carnations, snapdragons, or the Star of Bethlehem, next to buffet displays of fruits or vegetables, as they are extremely sensitive to the gasses emitted by food and will drop their flowers
- Avoid any flower that is too heavily scented, which can be distracting from the appetizing smell of the food

UNIQUE ALTERNATIVES

- Use whole fruits and bunches of berries
- Use artichokes for a summer wedding and figs or pumpkins for a fall/winter reception
- Vegetables can be shaped and cut into decorations

QUESTIONS FOR THE FLORIST

Use these questions to compare and contrast different florists you are considering.

BE SURE TO ASK

- What is the name of your company?

Option 1 ....

Option 2 ....

- What is your website?

Option 1 ....

Option 2 ....

- What is your e-mail?

Option 1 ....

Option 2 ....

- What is your address?

Option 1 ....

Option 2 ....

- What is the name of my contact person?

Option 1 ....

Option 2 ....

- What is his or her phone number?

Option 1 ....

Option 2 ....

BE SURE TO ASK CONT'D

- How many years have you been in business?

Option 1 ....

Option 2 ....

- What percentage of your business is dedicated to weddings?

Option 1 ....

Option 2 ....

- Do you have access to out-of-season flowers?

Option 1 ....

Option 2 ....

- Will you visit my wedding sites to make floral recommendations?

Option 1 ....

Option 2 ....

- Can you preserve my bridal bouquet?

Option 1 ....

Option 2 ....

- Do you rent vases and candleholders?

Option 1 ....

Option 2 ....

BE SURE TO ASK CONT'D

- What is the cost of the desired bridal bouquet?

Option 1 ....

Option 2 ....

- What is the cost of the desired boutonniere?

Option 1 ....

Option 2 ....

- What is the cost of the desired corsage?

Option 1 ....

Option 2 ....

- Do you have liability insurance?

Option 1 ....

Option 2 ....

- What are your delivery/setup fees?

Option 1 ....

Option 2 ....

- What is your payment policy?

Option 1 ....

Option 2 ....

- What is your cancellation policy?

Option 1 ....

Option 2 ....

FLOWERS BY SEASON

FLOWER	Winter	Spring	Summer	Fall
Allium		*	*	
Alstroemeria	*	*	*	*
Amaryllis	*		*	
Anemone	*	*		*
Aster	*	*	*	*
Baby's Breath	*	*	*	*
Bachelor's Button	*	*	*	*
Billy Buttons		*	*	
Bird of Paradise	*	*	*	*
Bouvardia	*	*	*	*
Calla Lily	*	*	*	*
Carnation	*	*	*	*
Celosia		*	*	
Chrysanthemum	*	*	*	*
Daffodils		*		
Dahlia			*	*
Delphinium			*	*
Eucalyptus	*	*	*	*
Freesia	*	*	*	*
Gardenia	*	*	*	*
Gerbera	*	*	*	*
Gladiolus	*	*	*	*
Iris	*	*	*	*
Liatris	*	*	*	*
Lily	*	*	*	*

FLOWERS BY SEASON CONT'D

FLOWER	Winter	Spring	Summer	Fall
Lily of the Valley		*		
Lisianthus		*	*	*
Narcissus	*	*		*
Nerine	*	*	*	*
Orchid (Cattleya)	*	*	*	*
Orchid (Cymbidium)	*	*	*	*
Peony		*		
Pincushion			*	
Protea	*			*
Queen Anne's Lace			*	
Ranunculas		*		
Rose	*	*	*	*
Saponaria			*	
Snapdragon		*	*	*
Speedwell			*	
Star of Bethlehem	*			*
Statice	*	*	*	*
Stephanotis	*	*	*	*
Stock	*	*	*	*
Sunflower		*	*	*
Sweet Pea		*		
Tuberose			*	*
Tulip	*	*		
Waxflower	*	*		

BOUQUETS & FLOWERS AT-A-GLANCE

Bride's Bouquet

Color Scheme:

Style:

Flowers:

Greenery:

Other (Ribbons, etc.):

Maid of Honor's Bouquet

Color Scheme:

Style:

Flowers:

Greenery:

Other (Ribbons, etc.):

Bridesmaids' Bouquet

Color Scheme:

Style:

Flowers:

Greenery:

Other (Ribbons, etc.):

BOUQUETS & FLOWERS AT-A-GLANCE CONT'D

Flower Girls' Bouquet

Color Scheme:..

Style: ....

Flowers: ....

Greenery:...

Other (Ribbons, etc.): ....

Corsages & Boutonnieres

- Groom's Boutonniere:

....

....

....

- Ushers' and Other Family Members' Boutonnieres:

....

....

- Mother of the Bride Corsage:

....

....

- Mother of the Groom Corsage:

....

....

BOUQUETS & FLOWERS AT-A-GLANCE CONT'D

Floral Arrangements

- Altar or Chuppah

....

....

- Steps to Altar or Chuppah

....

....

- Pews

....

....

- Entrance to the Ceremony

....

....

- Entrance to the Reception

....

....

- Receiving Line

....

....

BOUQUETS & FLOWERS AT-A-GLANCE CONT'D

Floral Arrangements

- Head Table

....

....

- Parents' Table

....

....

- Guest Table

....

....

- Cake Table

....

....

- Serving Table (Buffet, Dessert)

....

....

- Gift Table

....

....

FLORIST INFORMATION

Use this form to organize the information about your final florist selection.

FLORIST AT-A-GLANCE

- Company Name:
- Contact Person:
- Website:
- Email:
- Address:
- City:
- State/Zip Code:
- Phone Number:
- Payment Policy:
- Cancellation Policy:
- Delivery/Setup Time:
- Notes:

Transportation

Your wedding-day transportation can be a chance to showcase your personality, from renting a vintage car to arriving in style in a stretch limousine.

TRANSPORTATION

It is customary for the bride and her father to ride to the ceremony site together on the wedding day. You may also include some or all members of your wedding party.

OPTIONS

- Limousine
- Rent a classic car
- Rent a luxury car, such as a Mercedes or Ferrari
- Romantic horse-drawn carriage

THINGS TO CONSIDER

- Traditionally, the procession to the church begins with the bride's mother and several of the bride's attendants in the first vehicle
- If desired, you can provide a second vehicle for the rest of the attendants
- The bride and her father will go in the last vehicle
- Limousines sometimes book on a three-hour minimum basis
- Consider hiring only one large limousine to transport you, your parents, and your attendants to the ceremony, and then you and your new husband from the ceremony to the reception
- The bride may choose to ride in a large limo with just her wedding party

REMEMBER!

- Make sure the company you choose is fully licensed and has liability insurance
- Do not pay the full amount until after the event

QUESTIONS TO ASK ABOUT TRANSPORTATION

Use these questions to compare and contrast different transportation services you are considering.

BE SURE TO ASK

- What is the name of your company?

Option 1 ....

Option 2 ....

- What is your website?

Option 1 ....

Option 2 ....

- What is your e-mail?

Option 1 ....

Option 2 ....

- What is your address?

Option 1 ....

Option 2 ....

- What is the name of my contact person?

Option 1 ....

Option 2 ....

- What is his or her phone number?

Option 1 ....

Option 2 ....

BE SURE TO ASK CONT'D

✲ How many years have you been in business?

Option 1 ....

Option 2 ....

✲ How many vehicles do you have available?

Option 1 ....

Option 2 ....

✲ Can you provide a back-up vehicle?

Option 1 ....

Option 2 ....

✲ What types of vehicles are available?

Option 1 ....

Option 2 ....

✲ What are the various sizes of vehicles available?

Option 1 ....

Option 2 ....

✲ How old are the vehicles?

Option 1 ....

Option 2 ....

✲ How many drivers are available?

Option 1 ....

Option 2 ....

BE SURE TO ASK CONT'D

✼ Can you show me photos of your drivers?

Option 1 ....

Option 2 ....

✼ How do your drivers dress for weddings?

Option 1 ....

Option 2 ....

✼ Do you have liability insurance?

Option 1 ....

Option 2 ....

✼ What is the minimum rental time?

Option 1 ....

Option 2 ....

✼ What is the cost per hour? Two hours? Three hours?

Option 1 ....

Option 2 ....

✼ How much gratuity is expected?

Option 1 ....

Option 2 ....

✼ What is your payment/cancellation policy?

Option 1 ....

Option 2 ....

TRANSPORTATION TO CEREMONY SITE

Bride

Pickup Time/Location: ....

Vehicle/Driver: ....

Groom

Pickup Time/Location: ....

Vehicle/Driver: ....

Bride's Parents

Pickup Time/Location: ....

Vehicle/Driver: ....

Groom's Parents

Pickup Time/Location: ....

Vehicle/Driver: ....

Bridesmaids

Pickup Time/Location: ....

Vehicle/Driver: ....

Ushers

Pickup Time/Location: ....

Vehicle/Driver: ....

Other:

Pickup Time/Location: ....

Vehicle/Driver: ....

TRANSPORTATION TO RECEPTION SITE

❊ Bride

Pickup Time/Location: ....

Vehicle/Driver: ....

❊ Groom

Pickup Time/Location: ....

Vehicle/Driver: ....

❊ Bride's Parents

Pickup Time/Location: ....

Vehicle/Driver: ....

❊ Groom's Parents

Pickup Time/Location: ....

Vehicle/Driver: ....

❊ Bridesmaids

Pickup Time/Location: ....

Vehicle/Driver: ....

❊ Ushers

Pickup Time/Location: ....

Vehicle/Driver: ....

❊ Other:

Pickup Time/Location: ....

Vehicle/Driver: ....

TRANSPORTATION INFORMATION

Use this form to organize the information about your final transportation service provider.

TRANSPORTATION AT-A-GLANCE

- Company Name:...
- Contact Person:...
- Website:...
- Email:...
- Address:...
- City:...
- State/Zip Code:...
- Phone Number:...
- Payment Policy: ....
- Cancellation Policy:...
- Notes:...

....

....

....

....

....

Rental Items

Not all items for the ceremony and reception need to be purchased. Rental items also allow you to host a reception in your own home or in less traditional locations, such as an art museum, a local park, or a beach.

BRIDAL SLIP

The bridal slip is an undergarment which gives the bridal gown its proper shape.

THINGS TO CONSIDER

- Many bridal salons rent slips
- Be sure to wear the same slip you'll be wearing on your wedding day during your fittings
- Schedule an appointment to pick up your slip one week before the wedding; otherwise, you run the risk of not having one available on your wedding day
- If rented, the slip will have to be returned shortly after the wedding. Arrange for someone to do this for you within the allotted time

CEREMONY ACCESSORIES

Ceremony rental accessories are the additional items needed for the ceremony but not included in the ceremony site fee.

OPTIONS

- Aisle runner: A thin rug made of plastic, paper or cloth extending the length of the aisle
- Kneeling cushion: A small cushion or pillow placed in front of the altar where the bride and groom kneel for their wedding blessing
- Arch (Christian): A white lattice or brass arch where the bride and groom exchange their vows
- Chuppah (Jewish): A canopy under which a Jewish ceremony is performed, symbolizing cohabitation and consummation

- Audio equipment
- Aisle stanchions
- Candelabra
- Candles
- Candle-lighters
- Chairs
- Heaters
- Gift table
- Guest book stand
- Canopy

THINGS TO CONSIDER

- Check how long the rental supplier has been in business and their reputation
- Find out the company's payment, reservation, and cancellation policies
- Reserve the items you need well in advance
- Ask if the rental company will let you reserve emergency items, such as heaters or canopies, without having to pay for them unless you need them
- If someone else requests the items you have reserved, the company should give you the right of first refusal
- When planning a wedding at a home, consider that you will need to rent every piece of furniture, including tables and chairs, linens, silverware, and more

TIPS TO SAVE MONEY

- Negotiate a package deal by renting items for both the ceremony and the reception from the same supplier

TENT OR CANOPY

A large tent or canopy may be required for receptions held outdoors to protect you and your guests from the sun or rain.

THINGS TO CONSIDER

- You may need to rent several smaller canopies rather than one large one. Contact several party rental suppliers to discuss the options
- Consider this cost when making a decision between an outdoor and an indoor reception
- In cooler weather, heaters may also be necessary
- Usually rented through party rental suppliers, tents and canopies can be expensive due to the labor involved in delivery and setup

TIPS TO SAVE MONEY

- Shop early and compare prices with several suppliers

TABLES & CHAIRS

You will have to provide tables and chairs for your guests if your reception site or caterer doesn't provide them as part of their package.

OPTIONS

- White wooden or plastic chairs
- Most common tables are round and seat eight guests
- Most common head table arrangement is several rectangular tables placed end-to-end to seat your entire wedding party on one side, facing your guests

THINGS TO CONSIDER

- Contact various party rental suppliers to find out what types of chairs and tables they carry, as well as their price ranges
- When comparing prices of renting tables and chairs, include the cost of delivery and setup
- For a full meal, you will have to provide tables and seating for all guests
- For a cocktail reception, you only need to provide tables and chairs for approximately 30 to 50 percent of your guests

TIPS TO SAVE MONEY

- Attempt to negotiate free delivery and setup

LINENS & TABLEWARE

You will also need to rent linens and tableware for your reception if these are not provided as part of your package.

OPTIONS

- Sit-down: Tablecloth and complete place settings
- Buffet: Tables are covered with a cloth, but settings are not mandatory. Plates and silverware may be located at the buffet table, next to the food

THINGS TO CONSIDER

- Linens and tableware depend on the formality of your reception
- When comparing prices of linens and tableware, include the cost of delivery and setup
- Traditional table linens are white, but the color may be coordinated with the wedding

OTHER RENTAL ITEMS

You may need to purchase, rent, or borrow other miscellaneous items for your reception, such as heaters, lighting, trash cans, a gift table, trash bags, and so on.

OPTIONS

- Lanterns provide ambience for an evening reception
- Rent a dance floor if one is not included
- Rent heaters if your ceremony or reception will be held outdoors and if the temperature could drop below 65 degrees

THINGS TO CONSIDER

- Choose from fire lanterns to electric lanterns
- When comparing prices of dance floors, factor in the delivery and setup fees

THINGS TO CONSIDER CONT'D

- Choose from electric and gas heaters; however, gas heaters are more popular since they do not have unsightly and unsafe electric cords
- Factor in the cost of providing trash cans, a gift table, and trash bags

NOTES

QUESTIONS TO ASK RENTAL SUPPLIERS

Use these questions to compare and contrast different rental suppliers.

BE SURE TO ASK

- What is the name of your company?

Option 1 ....

Option 2 ....

- What is your website?

Option 1 ....

Option 2 ....

- What is your e-mail?

Option 1 ....

Option 2 ....

- What is your address?

Option 1 ....

Option 2 ....

- What is the name of my contact person?

Option 1 ....

Option 2 ....

- What is his or her phone number?

Option 1 ....

Option 2 ....

BE SURE TO ASK CONT'D

❊ What are your hours of operation?

Option 1 ....

Option 2 ....

❊ Do you have liability insurance?

Option 1 ....

Option 2 ....

❊ What is the cost per item needed?

Option 1 ....

Option 2 ....

❊ What is the cost of delivery/setup/pickup?

Option 1 ....

Option 2 ....

❊ When would items be delivered/set up/picked up?

Option 1 ....

Option 2 ....

❊ What is your payment policy?

Option 1 ....

Option 2 ....

❊ What is your cancellation policy?

Option 1 ....

Option 2 ....

CEREMONY EQUIPMENT INFORMATION

Use this form to organize the information about your final rental service provider for your ceremony.

RENTAL SUPPLIER: CEREMONY

- Company Name:
- Contact Person:
- Website:
- Email:
- Address:
- City:
- State/Zip Code:
- Phone Number:
- Payment Policy:
- Cancellation Policy:
- Delivery Time: Setup Time:
- Tear-Down Time: Pickup Time:
- Notes:

RENTAL ITEM CHECKLIST: CEREMONY

Qty	Item	Price	Total
....	Arch/Altar	$....................	$....................
....	Canopy (Chuppah)	$....................	$....................
....	Backdrops	$....................	$....................
....	Floor Candelabra	$....................	$....................
....	Candles	$....................	$....................
....	Candle Lighters	$....................	$....................
....	Kneeling Bench	$....................	$....................
....	Aisle Stanchions	$....................	$....................
....	Aisle Runners	$....................	$....................
....	Guest Book Stand	$....................	$....................
....	Gift Table	$....................	$....................
....	Chairs	$....................	$....................
....	Audio Equipment	$....................	$....................
....	Lighting	$....................	$....................
....	Heating/Cooling	$....................	$....................
....	Umbrellas/Tents	$....................	$....................
....	Bug Eliminator	$....................	$....................
....	Coat/Hat Rack	$....................	$....................
....	Garbage Cans	$....................	$....................

RECEPTION EQUIPMENT INFORMATION

Use this form to organize the information about your final rental service provider for your reception.

RENTAL SUPPLIER: RECEPTION

- Company Name:
- Contact Person:
- Website:
- Email:
- Address:
- City:
- State/Zip Code:
- Phone Number:
- Payment Policy:
- Cancellation Policy:
- Delivery Time: Setup Time:
- Tear-Down Time: Pickup Time:
- Notes:

RENTAL ITEM CHECKLIST: RECEPTION

Qty	Item	Price	Total
…………	Audio Equipment	$…………………	$…………………
…………	Cake Table	$…………………	$…………………
…………	Candelabras/Candles	$…………………	$…………………
…………	Canopies	$…………………	$…………………
…………	Coat/Hat Rack	$…………………	$…………………
…………	Dance Floor	$…………………	$…………………
…………	Bug Eliminator	$…………………	$…………………
…………	Garbage Cans	$…………………	$…………………
…………	Gift Table	$…………………	$…………………
…………	Guest Tables	$…………………	$…………………
…………	Heating/Cooling	$…………………	$…………………
…………	High/Booster Chairs	$…………………	$…………………
…………	Lighting	$…………………	$…………………
…………	Mirror Disco Ball	$…………………	$…………………
…………	Place Card Table	$…………………	$…………………
…………	Tents	$…………………	$…………………
…………	Umbrellas	$…………………	$…………………
…………	Visual Equipment	$…………………	$…………………
…………	Wheelchair Ramp	$…………………	$…………………

THINGS TO DO

- [ ]
- [ ]
- [ ]
- [ ]
- [ ]

NOTES

Gifts

Gifts are a wonderful way to show your appreciation to each other, members of your wedding party, and to all those who have assisted you in your wedding planning process.

BRIDE'S GIFT

The bride's gift is traditionally given by the groom to the bride. It is typically a personal gift, such as a piece of jewelry.

OPTIONS

- String of pearls
- Watch
- Pearl earrings
- Jewelry box
- Perfume
- Lingerie

GROOM'S GIFT

The groom's gift is given by the bride to the groom.

OPTIONS

- Watch
- Album of boudoir photos
- Golf clubs
- Electronics

BRIDESMAIDS' GIFT

Bridesmaids' gifts are given by the bride to her bridesmaids and Maid of Honor as a permanent keepsake of the wedding.

OPTIONS

- Certificate for a spa treatment before the wedding day
- Jewelry that can be worn during the wedding
- Jewelry boxes
- Pashminas or wraps
- Personalized sweat suits or tank tops
- Favorite beauty products
- Tote or cosmetic bags
- Customized stationery
- Framed photo of you and the bridesmaid

THINGS TO CONSIDER

- Present gifts at the bridesmaids' luncheon or the rehearsal dinner
- Maid of Honor's gift may be similar but a bit more expensive

TIPS TO SAVE MONEY

- Ask your photographer to take, at no extra charge, professional portraits of each bridesmaid and her escort to use as bridesmaids' gifts

GROOMSMEN'S GIFTS

Groomsmen's gifts are given by the groom to his ushers as a permanent keepsake of the wedding.

OPTIONS

- Money clip
- Wallets
- Cigars
- Watch
- Knives
- Flask
- Luxury shaving kit
- Bottle of fine wine

THINGS TO CONSIDER

- The groom should deliver his gifts to the groomsmen at the bachelor party or at the rehearsal dinner
- Best Man gift may be similar to the ushers' gifts, but should be a bit more expensive

TIPS TO SAVE MONEY

- Negotiate with your photographer to take, at no extra charge, professional portraits of each usher and his escort to use as ushers' gifts

WEDDING PARTY GIFTS

Bridesmaids

Item:

Qty: Price: $ Total: $

Maid of Honor

Item:

Qty: Price: $ Total: $

Ushers

Item:

Qty: Price: $ Total: $

Best Man

Item:

Qty: Price: $ Total: $

Flower Girl

Item:

Qty: Price: $ Total: $

Ring Bearer

Item:

Qty: Price: $ Total: $

Others:

Item:

Qty: Price: $ Total: $

Parties

Weddings are often much more than a day-long celebration. There are traditionally plenty of festivities before and even after the actual wedding day.

PARTIES CHECKLIST

Plan on making arrangements for the following events in addition to your ceremony and reception.

✔ **OPTIONS**

- ❑ Engagement party
- ❑ Bridal shower
- ❑ Bachelor party
- ❑ Bachelorette party
- ❑ Bridesmaids' luncheon
- ❑ Rehearsal dinner
- ❑ Day-after-wedding brunch

ENGAGEMENT PARTY

The engagement party is generally thrown by the bride's family to celebrate the big news.

THINGS TO CONSIDER

- An engagement party is traditionally held in your parents' home
- Consider renting a space or having dinner in a nice restaurant
- Gifts are not required at this party
- If your schedule or budget won't allow for it, an engagement party is by no means a requirement

BRIDAL SHOWER

Traditionally, your wedding shower is thrown by your Maid of Honor and bridesmaids (unless they are members of the immediate family). The agenda usually includes some games and gift-opening.

OPTIONS

- Traditional home event
- Tea party
- Spa day
- Cocktail party
- Themed event (lingerie, cooking, home decor)

THINGS TO CONSIDER

- Because a shower is a gift-giving occasion, it is not considered socially acceptable for anyone in your immediate family to host this event. If your mother or sisters wish to be involved, have them offer to help with the cost of the event or offer their home for it

- You may have several showers thrown for you. When creating your guest lists, be sure not to invite the same people to multiple showers

- Members of the wedding party can be invited to all showers without the obligation of bringing a gift

- The invitation should give guests an idea of the theme and what type of gift to bring

- Only include people who have been invited to the wedding. The only exception to this is a work shower, to which all coworkers may be invited

- Modernly, even men are being invited as coed showers become more and more popular

- Be sure to have someone keep track of which gift is from whom

BACHELOR PARTY

The bachelor party is a male-only affair typically organized by the Best Man. He is responsible for selecting the date and reserving the place and entertainment as well as inviting the groom's male friends and family. The ushers should also help with the organization of this party.

OPTIONS

- Dinner and drinks
- Golf
- Casino trip
- Cruise
- Attend a sporting event
- Brewery tour or tasting
- Rent a boat
- Skydiving
- Camping

THINGS TO CONSIDER

- The Best Man should ask the groom what kind of party he wants — wild or mild
- The Best Man should not plan your bachelor party for the night before the wedding. You don't want to have a hangover or be exhausted during your wedding
- It is much more appropriate to have the bachelor party two or three nights before the wedding
- Your Best Man should designate a driver for you and for those who will be drinking alcohol
- Consider using an Evite to give the group details

BACHELORETTE PARTY

The bachelorette party is typically organized by the Maid of Honor for the females in the wedding party.

OPTIONS

- Dinner and drinks
- Spa day
- Wine tasting
- Cruise
- Yoga or Pilates retreat
- Scavenger hunt
- Mini-vacation to the beach

THINGS TO CONSIDER

- The Maid of Honor should ask the bride what kind of party she wants — wild or mild

- Coordinate transportation for guests who are drinking

- Buy something for the bride to wear to make her stand out, such as a feather boa, tiara, or beads

- Don't havc thc party the day before the wedding. A few weeks before or another date when the whole party can get together is more appropriate

- Consider using an Evite to give the group details

BRIDESMAIDS' LUNCHEON

The bridesmaids' luncheon is given by the bride for her bridesmaids to thank them for their help. It is not a shower; rather, it is simply a time for good friends to get together formally.

OPTIONS

- Light lunch
- Tea party
- Picnic
- At-home get-together
- Salon for manicures and pedicures

THINGS TO CONSIDER

- Host the luncheon a day or two before the wedding
- You can give your bridesmaids their gifts at this gathering. Otherwise, plan to give them their gifts at the rehearsal dinner
- Say a few kind words about each bridesmaid and what her friendship has meant to you
- Often the bridesmaids will give the bride her traditional items, such as her "something borrowed," or a gift they have gotten her
- Ask your wedding party to share their wedding and relationships stories and offer advice

REHEARSAL DINNER

It is customary that the groom's parents host a dinner party following the rehearsal, the evening before the wedding. The dinner usually includes the bridal party, their spouses or guests, both sets of parents, close family members, the officiant, and the wedding consultant and/or coordinator.

OPTIONS

- Restaurant
- Hotel
- Private hall
- Groom's parents' home

THINGS TO CONSIDER

- Some couples invite all guests who have traveled in from out of town to the rehearsal
- Consider serving cocktails and hors d'oeuvres and inviting all your wedding guests in place of a sit-down dinner
- The bride and groom should take this time to thank their parents for the wedding. Keep the speech short and simple
- Take this chance to introduce your families and wedding parties to each other
- Make sure to mingle with any special guests as you may not have time to give them personal attention during the wedding reception

DAY-AFTER-WEDDING BRUNCH

Many times the newlyweds will want to host a brunch the day after the wedding to spend one last bit of time with their guests and to thank them for coming to the wedding. Brunch can be much less formal than the rest of the wedding. Ask your family to help create this casual get-together.

OPTIONS

- Use your caterer
- Have family cook
- Eat at the hotel where most guests are staying

THINGS TO CONSIDER

- Solicit family members to help cook or pick up brunch foods. A family member who still wants to contribute to your wedding is a perfect choice to host
- If many guests are at one hotel, consider having the brunch there. If the hotel offers a continental breakfast, ask the hotel to reserve space in the breakfast room for your group
- Consider keeping the brunch menu simple: have bagels, croissants, jams, fruit, coffee, and juice.
- Choose a reasonable time for the brunch: Not too early, as many guests will be recovering from the festivities of the reception, but not too late, as out-of-town guests will have travel arrangements to attend to

Planning a Green Wedding

Green or "eco-chic" weddings are quickly growing in popularity. Having a green wedding can make a statement to your guests about the importance of protecting the earth from wear and tear.

OPTIONS FOR A GREEN WEDDING

More wedding planners and vendors are offering green options! However, be aware that a green wedding can cost up to 20 percent cost more than a traditional wedding.

INVITATIONS

OPTIONS

- Invitations using organic or soy ink on recycled paper
- Plantable invitations
- Save paper by skipping multi-envelope invitations

OPTIONS CONT'D

- Use a postcard for your Save the Date
- Choose paper alternatives such as bamboo, hemp, banana stalks, and cotton

THINGS TO CONSIDER

- Oddly sized or shaped invitations will cost more in postage
- Always send a paper invitation; reserve Evites for the less-formal Save the Date
- Create a wedding website to give guests maps and details of events such as the bachelor/bachelorette parties, rehearsal dinner, and bridal shower

LOCATION

OPTIONS

- Have your wedding and reception in the same place to avoid wasting energy and natural resources on transportation
- Have the wedding outside, instead of in an energy-inefficient reception hall. Utilize the natural beauty of the site to have fewer wasteful decorations

THINGS TO CONSIDER

- Locate an LEED-certified space at www.usgbcorg. LEED stands for "Leadership in Energy and Environmental Design" and means the space is sustainable and conserves water, energy, and electricity using solar power, insulation panels, and other state-of-the-art technology

FLOWERS

OPTIONS

- Use potted plants; have your guests take them home as favors and reuse them
- Have plants and flowers donated to a local hospice or elderly care center after the wedding
- If you do want flowers, get organically grown flowers – meaning they are grown without pesticides or insecticides

THINGS TO CONSIDER

- Non-organic roses are actually sprayed with perfume
- Consider organic roses, which have real fragrance. Have your guests toss the organic rose petals as you walk down the aisle

THINGS TO CONSIDER CONT'D

- Get flowers from a local nursery to avoid using up natural resources during shipping
- Be aware that organic flowers won't last as long, however, so make sure your florist considers timing

ON THE TABLE

OPTIONS

- Choose an organic menu, with seasonal or locally grown products to avoid shipping costs
- Choose organic wine or beer. Make sure they are registered with the USDA National Organic Program
- Use recycled napkins and table linens
- Use natural products for placecards, such as leaves or river stones. Give out plantable or biodegradable favors to reduce waste
- Choose beeswax or soy-based candles over those made with petroleum, a non-earth friendly product
- For the serious eco-friendly couple, request biodegradable utensils and plates — made out of potatoes, cornstarch, or sugarcane. Then have them composted after the wedding!

THINGS TO CONSIDER

- An organic menu can raise costs by 10 percent
- You will be hard-pressed to find an all-organic caterer, so instruct your caterer to shop at local farmer's markets and choose fresh, seasonal ingredients
- Be aware that with a seasonal menu, it's not likely you'll be able to taste the menu ahead of time so find someone you really trust
- Donate any extra food to a homeless shelter

GOWN & TUX

OPTIONS

- Purchase a secondhand or vintage gown. Have it altered to look more modern and to fit your body perfectly
- Consider borrowing a gown from a family member or close friend
- Purchase a gown made of organic fabrics or with eco-friendly dyes
- The groom can wear a hemp tux

THINGS TO CONSIDER

- Be cautious buying a secondhand gown online. Ask for details and photos. Pay with a credit card in case there is a dispute
- Have your bridesmaids choose their own gowns so they can choose a dress they will wear again
- Donate your gown after the ceremony

RINGS

OPTIONS

- Buy a conflict-free diamond — one not mined to help fund finance arms purchases. Be sure to ask for certified conflict-free diamonds
- Get a vintage piece
- Have an old piece of jewelry melted down and made into a new ring

THINGS TO CONSIDER

- Consider a wooden ring. They're custom-made and inexpensive (a few hundred dollars)

GIFTS

OPTIONS

- Create a registry where guests donate to a favorite charity instead of buying you gifts
- Register for a home-delivery service that delivers organic food products
- Ask for national park passes
- Ask for home-gardening tools to grow your own fruits and vegetables

THINGS TO CONSIDER

- If you ask guests to donate to a charity organization, avoid something political; stick to organizations that benefit international aid, nature, animals, disease prevention, or relief efforts
- Remind guests that any charitable contribution is tax-deductible
- Expect that some guests will still feel more comfortable bringing a traditional gift

HONEYMOON

✔ OPTIONS

- Go on a volunteer trip — build houses for Habitat for Humanity or help the Red Cross
- Take an eco-friendly or low-impact honeymoon, and stay in a green resort
- Go camping

✔ THINGS TO CONSIDER

- Request accommodations that hold "Green Globe" certification, like Sandals Jamaica
- For U.S. honeymoons, visit www.greenhotels.com for listings of eco-friendly hotels in each state
- Be aware that a green honeymoon may mean sacrificing some luxuries, such as TV and Internet

TRAVEL & CARBON EMISSIONS

✔ OPTIONS

- Use an online "wedding carbon footprint calculator" to determine the amount of greenhouse gases and carbon emissions that will be generated by guests flying and driving into town

✔ OPTIONS CONT'D

- Purchase "carbon credits" from www.terrapass.com, which put money toward U.S. carbon-reducing energy projects, to help offset the environmental damage of the wedding

✔ THINGS TO CONSIDER

- Carbon dioxide emissions from guest travel are the single biggest environmental impact from your wedding. Keep emissions and effects on the environment low by having a smaller wedding

THINGS TO DO

- [ ]
- [ ]
- [ ]
- [ ]
- [ ]

NOTES

Miscellaneous

With all that is involved in planning a wedding, it is easy to forget some simple but important tasks. Make arrangements for the following aspects in addition to your ceremony and reception.

MARRIAGE LICENSE

You will be required to sign a marriage license before you can be legally considered husband and wife.

OPTIONS

- Some states (California and Nevada, for example) offer two types of marriage licenses: a public license and a confidential one
- The public license is the most common one and requires a health certificate and a blood test. It can only be obtained at the County Clerk's office

OPTIONS CONT'D

- The confidential license is usually less expensive and does not require a health certificate or blood test. If offered, it can usually be obtained from most Justices of the Peace

THINGS TO CONSIDER

- An oath must be taken in order to receive either license
- Requirements vary from state to state, but generally include the following points:
    - Applying for and paying the fee for the marriage license. There is usually a waiting period before the license is valid and a limited time before it expires
    - Meeting residency requirements for the state and/or county where the ceremony will take place
    - Meeting the legal age requirements for both bride and groom or having parental consent
    - Presenting any required identification, birth or baptismal certificates, marriage eligibility, or other documents
    - Obtaining a medical examination and/or blood test for both the bride and groom to detect communicable diseases

PRENUPTIAL AGREEMENT

A prenuptial agreement is a legal contract between the bride and groom itemizing the property each brings into the marriage and explaining how those properties will be divided in case of divorce or death.

OPTIONS

- Although you can write your own agreement, it is wise for an attorney to draw up or review the document
- You should be represented by different attorneys

THINGS TO CONSIDER

- Consider a prenuptial agreement if one or both of you have a significant amount of capital or assets, or if there are children involved from a previous marriage
- If you are going to live in a different state after the wedding, have an attorney from that state draw up or review your document
- Consider drawing up/reviewing your wills at this time

TIPS TO SAVE MONEY

- Some software packages allow you to write your own will and prenuptial agreement, saving you substantial attorney's fees. However, you should still have an attorney review it

BRIDAL GOWN PRESERVATION

Gowns are preserved to be protected from yellowing or getting damaged over the years. The pride and joy you will experience in seeing your daughter and/or granddaughter wear your wedding gown on her wedding day will more than justify the expense of having your gown preserved.

OPTIONS

- Bring your gown to a reputable dry cleaning company that specializes in preserving wedding gowns. They will dry clean your dress, vacuum seal it, and place it in an attractive box
- Some bridal boutiques offer gown preservation
- Most boxes have a plastic see-through window where you can show the top part of your dress to friends and family members without having to open the vacuum-sealed container

TIPS TO SAVE MONEY

- Try to negotiate having your gown preserved for free with the purchase of a wedding gown. Get any agreement in writing and be sure to have it signed by either the owner or the manager of the boutique

WEDDING CONSULTANT

Wedding consultants are professionals whose training, expertise, and contacts will help make your wedding as close to perfect as it can possibly be. They can save you considerable time, money, and stress when planning your wedding. You can have a wedding consultant help you do as much or as little as you think necessary.

OPTIONS

- Hire a consultant to help you plan the whole event from the beginning to the end, helping you formulate a budget, and select your ceremony and reception site, flowers, wedding gown, invitations, and service providers
- Hire a wedding consultant for coordinating the rehearsal and the wedding day only

THINGS TO CONSIDER

- A wedding consultant is part of your wedding budget, not an extra expense
- A good consultant should be able to save you at least the amount of his or her fee by suggesting less expensive alternatives that still enhance your wedding
- Wedding consultants have information on many ceremony and reception sites as well as reliable service providers, which will save you hours of investigation and legwork

THINGS TO CONSIDER CONT'D

- Many consultants obtain discounts from the service providers they work with
- You may get better service with a consultant; recommended service providers will go out of their way to do an excellent job for you so that the wedding consultant will continue to recommend their services
- A consultant should serve as an intermediary between you and your parents and/or service providers
- Check every consultant's references
- Ask the consultant if he or she is a member of the Association of Bridal Consultants (ABC) and ask to see a current membership certificate. All ABC members agree to uphold a Code of Ethics and Standards of Membership
- Ask if each consultant has formal training and experience in event planning and in other specialties related to weddings, such as flower arranging and catering

REMEMBER!

- You want to feel like a guest at your own wedding. You and your family should not have to worry about any details on that special day. This is the wedding consultant's job!

QUESTIONS TO ASK WEDDING CONSULTANTS

Use these questions to compare and contrast different wedding consultants.

BE SURE TO ASK

- What is the name of your company?

Option 1 ....

Option 2 ....

- What is your website?

Option 1 ....

Option 2 ....

- What is your e-mail?

Option 1 ....

Option 2 ....

- What is your address?

Option 1 ....

Option 2 ....

- How many years have you been in business?

Option 1 ....

Option 2 ....

- Are you a Association of Bridal Consultants member?

Option 1 ....

Option 2 ....

BE SURE TO ASK CONT'D

- What services do you provide?

Option 1 ....

Option 2 ....

- What are your hourly fees?

Option 1 ....

Option 2 ....

- Fee for complete wedding planning?

Option 1 ....

Option 2 ....

- Fee to oversee the rehearsal and wedding day?

Option 1 ....

Option 2 ....

- What is your payment policy?

Option 1 ....

Option 2 ....

- What is your cancellation policy?

Option 1 ....

Option 2 ....

- Other:

Option 1 ....

Option 2 ....

WEDDING PLANNING ONLINE

With a computer and an internet connection, you can ease the process of planning your wedding.

OPTIONS

- A good wedding planning website will help you create a budget, select your service providers, generate a guest list, address invitations and create a wedding timeline
- Keep track of payments made, invitations sent, RSVPs, gifts received, and much more
- Create your registry or design a personal web page or website all about your wedding
- WeddingSolutions.com allows you to create a wedding website, use online planning tools, provide details and updates to your wedding party, and more
- WedSpace.com is a social networking site that allows you to interact with other engaged couples, your guests, and wedding vendors. You can post photos, share ideas, get planning advice, and keep your guests updated on your wedding plans

TAXES

Don't forget to figure in the cost of taxes on all taxable items you purchase for your wedding. Many people make a big mistake by not figuring out the taxes they will have to pay for their wedding expenses.

THINGS TO CONSIDER

- Find out what the sales tax is in your area and which items are taxable and figure this expense into your overall budget
- For example, for a reception for 250 guests with an estimated cost of $60 per person, your pretax expenses would be $15,000. A sales tax of 7.5 percent would mean an additional expense of $1,125

CHANGE OF NAME/ADDRESS

If you have chosen to change your name, you will need to update your information and address for the following:

CHECKLIST

- ❑ Auto Insurance
- ❑ Auto Registration
- ❑ Bank Accounts
- ❑ Credit Cards
- ❑ Dentist
- ❑ Doctors
- ❑ Driver's License
- ❑ Employee Records
- ❑ Insurance: Dental
- ❑ Insurance: Disability
- ❑ Insurance: Home
- ❑ Insurance: Life
- ❑ Insurance: Renter's
- ❑ IRA Accounts
- ❑ Leases
- ❑ Loan Companies
- ❑ Magazines
- ❑ Memberships
- ❑ Mortgage
- ❑ Newspaper
- ❑ Passport
- ❑ Pensions
- ❑ Post Office
- ❑ Property Title
- ❑ Retirement Accounts
- ❑ Safe Deposit Box
- ❑ School Records
- ❑ Social Security
- ❑ Stockbroker
- ❑ Taxes
- ❑ Telephone Company
- ❑ Utilities
- ❑ Voter Registration
- ❑ Will/Trust

THINGS TO DO

- ❑
- ❑
- ❑
- ❑
- ❑

NOTES

Do's & Don'ts

If you can handle planning your wedding with your fiancé and parents, you can handle anything! Here is a list of do's and don'ts to follow for your Big Day.

WEDDING DO'S

Make your wedding planning easy, stress free, and memorable by accomplishing the following items.

DO'S

- Hire a professional wedding consultant
- Maintain a sense of humor
- Maintain open communication with your fiancé and with both sets of parents, especially if they are financing the wedding

DO'S CONT'D

- Be flexible and keep your overall budget in mind
- Maintain a regular routine of exercise and eat a well-balanced diet
- Buy *Wedding Party Responsibility Cards*, published by Wedding Solutions Publishing, and give a card to each member of your wedding party
- Register for gifts; consider a price range that your guests can afford
- Break in your shoes well before your wedding day
- Practice with makeup and various hairstyles for your wedding day
- Check recent references for all of your service providers
- Get everything in writing with your service providers
- Assign your guests to tables and group them together by age, interests, acquaintances, etc.
- Consider drawing up a prenuptial agreement and will
- Send thank-you notes as soon as you receive gifts
- Give a rose to each of your mothers as you walk down the aisle during the recessional

DO'S CONT'D

- Try to spend some time with each of your guests and personally thank them for coming to your wedding
- Encourage the bride's parents to introduce their family and friends to the family and friends of the groom's family, and vice versa
- Toast both sets of parents at the rehearsal dinner and/or at the reception. Thank them for everything they have done for you and for giving you a beautiful wedding
- Have a member of the wedding party set aside food for you if you are both too busy to eat much during the reception
- Keep a smile on your face; there will be many photographs taken of both of you
- Expect things to go wrong on your wedding day. Most likely if something does go wrong, no one will notice it but yourself. Relax and don't let it bother you
- Preserve the top tier of your wedding cake for your first year anniversary
- Send a special gift to both sets of parents, such as a small album containing the best photographs of the wedding. Personalize this gift by having it engraved with your names and the date of your wedding

WEDDING DON'TS

Avoid the following circumstances that may make your wedding planning more complicated than it needs to be.

DON'TS

- Don't get involved in other activities; you will be very busy planning your wedding
- Don't make any major decisions without discussing it openly with your fiancé
- Don't be controlling. Be open to other people's ideas
- Don't overspend your budget; you don't want to begin your life together in debt!
- Don't wait until the last minute to hire service providers. The good ones get booked months in advance
- Don't try to make everyone happy; it is impossible and will only make your wedding planning more difficult.
- Don't try to impress your friends
- Don't invite old boyfriends or girlfriends to your wedding, unless both you and your fiancé are friendly with them; you don't want to make anybody uncomfortable
- Don't try to do everything. Delegate responsibilities to your fiancé, your parents, and to members of your wedding party

DON'TS CONT'D

- Don't rely on friends or family to photograph or videotape your wedding. Hire professionals!
- Don't assume that members of your wedding party know what to do. Give them direction with the *Wedding Party Responsibility Cards*, available at most major bookstores
- Don't assume your service providers know what to do. Give each of them a copy of a detailed timeline
- Don't schedule your bachelor or bachelorette party the night before the wedding. You don't want to have a hangover on your special day!
- Don't arrive late to the ceremony!
- Don't drink too much during the reception; you don't want to make a fool of yourself on your most special day!
- Don't flirt with members of the opposite sex
- Don't allow your guests to drive drunk after the reception; you may be held responsible
- Don't rub cake in your spouse's face during the cake-cutting ceremony; he or she might not appreciate it!
- Don't overeat; this may upset your stomach or make you sleepy

DONT'S CONT'D

- Don't get too busy to eat. Have someone in your wedding party set aside plates of food for both of you
- Don't forget to give your DJ a music timeline
- Don't leave your reception without saying good-bye to your family and friends

NOTES

Wedding Traditions

In this section we discuss the origin, symbolism, and historical significance of some of the most popular wedding traditions.

POPULAR WEDDING TRADITIONS

Bride's bouquet

- Carried for protective reasons — it was thought to drive away evil spirits that might plague the wedding
- Symbolizes fertility and the hope for a large family
- Each flower was assigned a particular meaning when carried in a bride's bouquet

Bride's veil

- Historically symbolized virginity and innocence
- Protected bride from evil spirits
- Arranged marriages were common and often couples were not to officially meet until after the wedding

POPULAR WEDDING TRADITIONS CONT'D

Rice and petals

- Aids with fertility and the couple's harvest

Something old, Something new, Something borrowed, Something blue

- Old: Carried to represent the history of the bride and ties her to her family
- New: Represents the future and the bride's ties to her new family
- Borrowed: Should come from someone who is happily married and is carried in the hopes that their good fortune may rub off on you
- Blue: The color of purity and is carried to represent faithfulness in the marriage

White aisle runner

- Symbolizes bringing God into your union
- Indicative of walking on holy ground

Special seating for the families

- Traditionally seated on opposite sides of the church, because in ancient times families would often have a wedding in order to bring peace to warring clans

Groom entering first

- Groom enters first and gives his vows first, because he is considered to be the one who has initiated the wedding

POPULAR WEDDING TRADITIONS CONT'D

Father of the bride walking down the aisle

- Brides were literally given away by their fathers—women were betrothed, often at birth, to men they did not know, and their parents were able to "give them away"
- A way for the bride's family to publicly show their support of the union

Bride standing on the left

- The bride was placed on the groom's left in order to leave his sword-hand free in case he had to defend her

Wedding rings

- The circle of the wedding ring represents eternal love and devotion
- The Greeks believed that the fourth finger on the left hand has a vein which leads directly to the heart, so this is the finger onto which we place these bands

Kissing the bride

- During the Roman empire, the kiss between a couple symbolized a legal bond — hence the expression "sealed with a kiss"
- Based on the deeply rooted idea of the kiss as a vehicle for transference of power and souls

Couple being pronounced husband and wife

- Establishes their change of names and a definite point in time for the beginning of the marriage
- Remove any doubt in the minds of the couple or the witnesses concerning the validity of the marriage

POPULAR WEDDING TRADITIONS CONT'D

Signing the wedding papers

- To establish a public document and a continuing public record of the covenant

Signing the guest book

- Guests are official witnesses to the covenant. By signing the guest book, they are saying, "I have witnessed the vows, and I will testify to the reality of this marriage"
- Because of this significance, the guest book should be signed after the wedding rather than before it

The receiving line

- The receiving line is for guests to give their blessings to the couple and their parents

Feeding cake to each other

- This represents the sharing of their body to become one. A New Testament illustration of this symbolism is The Lord's Supper

Wedding Formations

The following section illustrates the typical ceremony formations for both Christian and Jewish weddings, as well as the typical formations for the receiving line, head table, and parents' tables at the reception.

CEREMONY FORMATIONS

Religious tradition, venue, and the formality of your wedding will dictate your ceremony formations. Depending on the size of your wedding parties on each side, your attendants may walk down the aisle alone or in male-female pairs. The wedding parties on the bride and groom's side do not have to be completely symmetrical, however, many churches and temples do have rules about how the wedding parties must line up during the ceremony.

You will practice your formations at the ceremony rehearsal, but you may also want to give each member of the wedding party a diagram so they know where to stand.

CHRISTIAN CEREMONY

Altar Line Up

Bride's Pews

Groom's Pews

ABBREVIATIONS

B=Bride
GF=Groom's Father
G=Groom
GM=Groom's Mother
BM=Best Man
BMa=Bridesmaids
MH=Maid of Honor
U=Ushers
BF=Bride's Father
FG=Flower Girl
BMo=Bride's Mother
RB=Ring Bearer
O=Officiant

CHRISTIAN CEREMONY

PROCESSIONAL

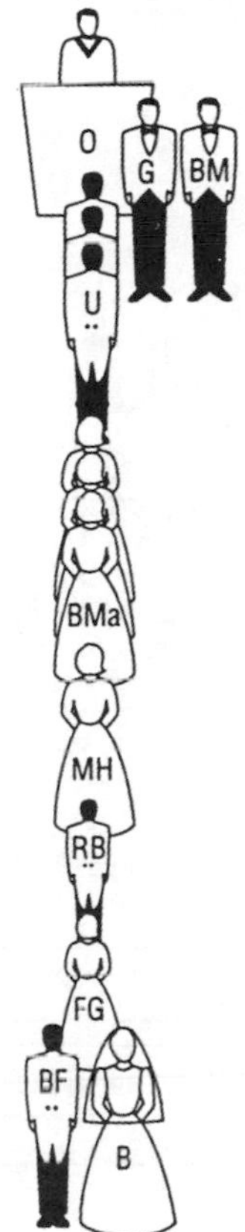

RECESSIONAL

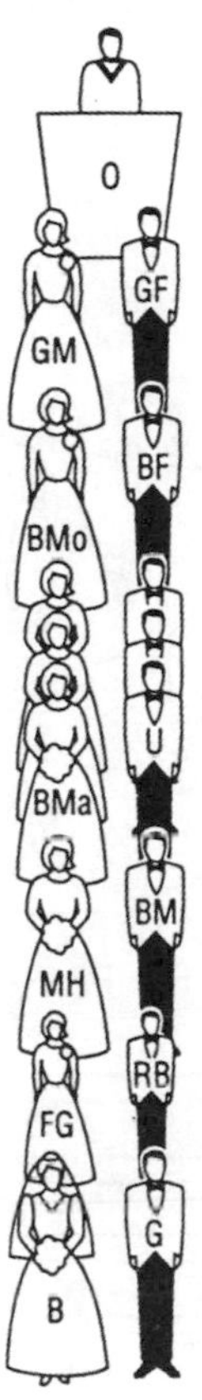

ABBREVIATIONS

B=Bride
GF=Groom's Father
G=Groom
GM=Groom's Mother
BM=Best Man
BMa=Bridesmaids
MH=Maid of Honor
U=Ushers
BF=Bride's Father
FG=Flower Girl
BMo=Bride's Mother
RB=Ring Bearer
O=Officiant

JEWISH CEREMONY

Altar Line Up

ABBREVIATIONS

B=Bride
GF=Groom's Father
G=Groom
GM=Groom's Mother
BM=Best Man
BMa=Bridesmaids
MH=Maid of Honor
U=Ushers
BF=Bride's Father
FG=Flower Girl
BMo=Bride's Mother
RB=Ring Bearer
R=Rabbi

JEWISH CEREMONY

PROCESSIONAL **RECESSIONAL**

ABBREVIATIONS

B=Bride
GF=Groom's Father
G=Groom
GM=Groom's Mother
BM=Best Man
BMa=Bridesmaids
MH=Maid of Honor
U=Ushers
BF=Bride's Father
FG=Flower Girl
BMo=Bride's Mother
RB=Ring Bearer
R=Rabbi

FORMATIONS

Receiving Line

Head Table

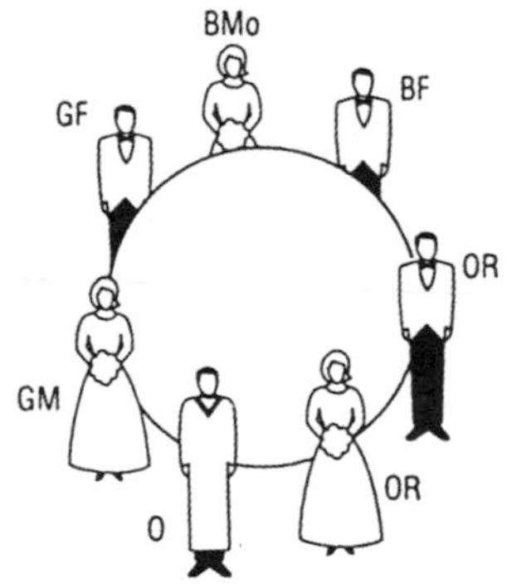

ABBREVIATIONS

B=Bride
GF=Groom's Father
G=Groom
GM=Groom's Mother
BM=Best Man
BMa=Bridesmaids
MH=Maid of Honor
U=Ushers
BF=Bride's Father
OR=Other Relatives
BMo=Bride's Mother
O=Officiant

Wedding Party Responsibilities

Each member of your wedding party has his or her individual duties and responsibilities. When each person knows what is expected of them, your wedding day will go off without a hitch!

MAID OF HONOR

- Helps bride select attire and address invitations
- Plans bridal shower
- Arrives at dressing site two hours before ceremony to assist bride in dressing
- Arrives dressed at ceremony site one hour before the wedding for photographs
- Arranges the bride's veil and train before the processional and recessional
- Holds bride's bouquet and groom's ring, if no ring bearer, during the ceremony
- Witnesses the signing of the marriage license
- Keeps bride on schedule
- Dances with Best Man during the bridal party dance

MAID OF HONOR CONT'D

- Helps bride change into her going away clothes
- Mails wedding announcements after the wedding
- Returns bridal slip, if rented

BEST MAN

- Responsible for organizing ushers' activities
- Organizes bachelor party for groom
- Drives groom to ceremony site and sees that he is properly dressed before the wedding
- Arrives dressed at ceremony site one hour before the wedding for photographs
- Brings marriage license to wedding
- Pays the clergyman, musicians, photographer, and any other service providers the day of the wedding
- Holds the bride's ring for the groom, if no ring bearer, until needed by officiant
- Witnesses the signing of the marriage license
- Drives newlyweds to reception, if no hired driver
- Offers first toast at reception, usually before dinner
- Keeps groom on schedule
- Dances with Maid of Honor during the bridal party dance
- May drive couple to airport or honeymoon suite
- Oversees return of tuxedo rentals for groom and ushers, on time and in good condition

BRIDESMAIDS

- Assist Maid of Honor in planning bridal shower
- Assist bride with errands and addressing invitations
- Participate in all pre-wedding parties
- Arrive at dressing site two hours before ceremony
- Arrive dressed at ceremony site one hour before the wedding for photographs
- Walk behind ushers in order of height during the processional, either in pairs or in single file
- Sit next to ushers at the head table
- Dance with ushers and other important guests
- Encourage single women to participate in the bouquet-tossing ceremony

USHERS

- Help Best Man with bachelor party
- Arrive dressed at ceremony site one hour before the wedding for photographs
- Distribute wedding programs and maps to guests
- Seat guests at the ceremony as follows:
  - If female, offer right arm/if male, walk to the left
  - If couple, offer right arm to female; male follows a step or two behind
  - Seat bride's guests in left pews
  - Seat groom's guests in right pews
  - Maintain equal number of guests in left/right pews
  - If a group of guests arrive at the same time, seat the eldest woman first
  - Just prior to the processional, escort groom's mother to her seat; then escort bride's mother to her seat

USHERS CONT'D

- Two ushers may roll carpet down the aisle after both mothers are seated
- If pew ribbons are used, two ushers may loosen them one row at a time after the ceremony
- Direct guests to the reception site
- Dance with bridesmaids and other important guests

BRIDE'S MOTHER

- Helps prepare guest list for bride and her family
- Helps plan the wedding ceremony and reception
- Helps bride select her bridal gown
- Helps bride keep track of gifts received
- Selects her own attire according to the formality and color of the wedding
- Makes accommodations for bride's out-of-town guests
- Arrives dressed at ceremony site one hour before the wedding for photographs
- Is the last person to be seated right before the processional begins
- Sits in the left front pew to the left of bride's father during the ceremony
- May stand up to signal the start of the processional
- Can witness the signing of the marriage license
- Dances with the groom after the first dance
- Acts as hostess at the reception

BRIDE'S MOTHER CONT'D

- Helps prepare guest list for bride and her family
- Helps plan the wedding ceremony and reception
- Helps bride select her bridal gown
- Helps bride keep track of gifts received
- Selects her own attire according to the formality and color of the wedding
- Makes accommodations for bride's out-of-town guests
- Arrives dressed at ceremony site one hour before the wedding for photographs
- Is the last person to be seated right before the processional begins
- Sits in the left front pew to the left of bride's father during the ceremony
- May stand up to signal the start of the processional
- Can witness the signing of the marriage license
- Dances with the groom after the first dance
- Acts as hostess at the reception

BRIDE'S FATHER

- Helps prepare guest list for bride and her family
- Selects attire that complements groom's attire
- Rides to the ceremony with bride in limousine
- Arrives dressed at ceremony site one hour before the wedding for photographs
- After giving bride away, sits in the left front pew to the right of bride's mother
- If divorced, sits in second or third row unless financing the wedding

BRIDE'S FATHER CONT'D

- When officiant asks, "Who gives this bride away?" answers, "Her mother and I do," or something similar
- Can witness the signing of the marriage license
- Dances with bride after first dance
- Acts as host at the reception

GROOM'S MOTHER

- Helps prepare guest list for groom and his family
- Selects attire that complements mother of the bride's attire
- Makes accommodation arrangements for groom's out-of-town guests
- With groom's father, plans rehearsal dinner
- Arrives dressed at ceremony site one hour before the wedding for photographs
- May stand up to signal the start of the processional
- Can witness the signing of the marriage license

GROOM'S FATHER

- Helps prepare guest list for groom and his family
- Selects attire that complements groom's attire
- With groom's mother, plans rehearsal dinner
- Offers toast to bride at rehearsal dinner
- Arrives dressed at ceremony site one hour before the wedding for photographs
- Can witness the signing of the marriage license

FLOWER GIRL

- Usually between the ages of 4 and 8
- Attends rehearsal to practice, but is not required to attend pre-wedding parties
- Arrives dressed at ceremony site 45 minutes before the wedding for photos
- Carries a basket filled with loose rose petals to strew along bride's path during processional, if allowed by ceremony site
- If very young, may sit with her parents during ceremony

RING BEARER

- Usually between the ages of 4 and 8
- Attends rehearsal to practice but is not required to attend pre-wedding parties
- Arrives at ceremony site 45 minutes before the wedding for photographs
- Carries a white pillow with rings attached
- If younger than seven years, carries mock rings
- If very young, may sit with his parents during ceremony
- If mock rings are used, turns the ring pillow over at the end of the ceremony

THINGS TO DO

- [ ]
- [ ]
- [ ]
- [ ]
- [ ]

NOTES

Who Pays for What

Use the following lists to determine the financial responsibilities for the bride and groom's sides, and all the members of the wedding party.

BRIDE AND/OR BRIDE'S FAMILY

- Engagement party
- Wedding consultant's fee
- Bridal gown, veil, and accessories
- Wedding stationery, calligraphy, and postage
- Wedding gift for bridal couple
- Groom's wedding ring
- Gifts for bridesmaids
- Bridesmaids' bouquets
- Pre-wedding parties and bridesmaids' luncheon
- Photography and videography
- Bride's medical exam and blood test

BRIDE AND/OR BRIDE'S FAMILY CONT'D

- Wedding guest book and other accessories
- Total cost of the ceremony, including location, flowers, music, rental items, and accessories
- Total cost of the reception, including location, flowers, music, rental items, accessories, food, beverages, cake, decorations, favors, etc.
- Transportation for bridal party to and from ceremony and reception
- Own attire and travel expenses

GROOM AND/OR GROOM'S FAMILY

- Own travel expenses and attire
- Rehearsal dinner
- Wedding gift for bridal couple
- Bride's wedding ring
- Gifts for groom's attendants
- Medical exam for groom including blood test
- Bride's bouquet and going away corsage
- Mothers' and grandmothers' corsages
- All boutonnieres
- Officiant's fee
- Marriage license
- Honeymoon expenses

ATTENDANTS

- Own attire except flowers
- Travel expenses
- Bridal shower/bachelorette paid for by Maid of Honor and bridesmaids
- Bachelor party paid for by Best Man and ushers

THINGS TO DO

- ❑
- ❑
- ❑
- ❑
- ❑

NOTES

Things to Bring

Pack the following items to make sure you have everything you need for your rehearsal and wedding day.

TO THE REHEARSAL

BRIDE'S LIST

- ❑ Wedding announcements (give to Maid of Honor to mail after wedding)
- ❑ Bridesmaids' gifts (if not already given)
- ❑ Camera and film
- ❑ Fake bouquet or ribbon bouquet from bridal shower
- ❑ Groom's gift (if not already given)
- ❑ Reception maps and wedding programs
- ❑ Rehearsal information and ceremony formations
- ❑ Flower girl basket and ring bearer pillow
- ❑ Seating diagrams for head table and parents' tables
- ❑ Wedding schedule of events/timeline
- ❑ CD/digital music player with wedding music

TO THE REHEARSAL

GROOM'S LIST

- ❑ Bride's gift (if not already given)
- ❑ Marriage license
- ❑ Ushers' gifts (if not already given)
- ❑ Service providers' fees to give to Best Man or wedding consultant so he or she can pay them at the wedding

TO THE CEREMONY

BRIDE'S LIST

- ❑ Aspirin
- ❑ Alka Seltzer
- ❑ Bobby pins
- ❑ Breath spray/mints
- ❑ Bridal gown
- ❑ Bridal gown box
- ❑ Cake knife
- ❑ Going away clothes
- ❑ Clear nail polish
- ❑ Deodorant
- ❑ Garter
- ❑ Gloves
- ❑ Groom's ring
- ❑ Guest book
- ❑ Hairbrush
- ❑ Hair spray
- ❑ Headpiece
- ❑ Iron
- ❑ Jewelry
- ❑ Kleenex
- ❑ Lint brush
- ❑ Luggage
- ❑ Makeup
- ❑ Mirror
- ❑ Nail polish
- ❑ Panty hose
- ❑ Passport
- ❑ Perfume
- ❑ Personal camera
- ❑ Plume pen for guest book
- ❑ Powder
- ❑ Purse
- ❑ Safety pins
- ❑ Scotch tape/masking tape
- ❑ Sewing kit
- ❑ Shoes

BRIDE'S LIST CONT'D

- ❑ Something old
- ❑ Something new
- ❑ Something borrowed
- ❑ Something blue
- ❑ Sixpence for shoe
- ❑ Spot remover
- ❑ Straight pins
- ❑ Tampons/pads
- ❑ Toasting goblets
- ❑ Toothbrush and paste

GROOM'S LIST

- ❑ Airline tickets
- ❑ Announcements
- ❑ Aspirin
- ❑ Alka Seltzer
- ❑ Breath spray/mints
- ❑ Bride's ring
- ❑ Going away clothes
- ❑ Cologne
- ❑ Cuff links
- ❑ Cummerbund
- ❑ Deodorant
- ❑ Hair comb
- ❑ Hair product
- ❑ Kleenex
- ❑ Lint brush
- ❑ Luggage
- ❑ Neck tie
- ❑ Passport
- ❑ Shirt
- ❑ Shoes
- ❑ Socks
- ❑ Toothbrush and paste
- ❑ Tuxedo
- ❑ Underwear

THINGS TO DO

- [ ]
- [ ]
- [ ]
- [ ]
- [ ]

NOTES

Honeymoon

Your honeymoon is the time to celebrate your new life together as a married couple. It should be the vacation of a lifetime.

HONEYMOON PLANNING

The honeymoon is traditionally the groom's responsibility. However, the planning of your honeymoon should be a joint decision as to where to go, how long to stay, and how much money to spend. You should start planning your honeymoon months before the wedding.

TRADITIONAL HONEYMOONS

CRUISES

- Typically, almost everything is included in the cost of your cruise: dining, unlimited group and individual activities, relaxing days and lively nights
- Costs vary greatly depending on the location the cruise will visit (if any) and your cabin accommodations

CRUISES CONT'D

- Pay attention to things like noisy areas and busy pathways when you choose a cabin
- Be sure to ask about extra costs, such as alcoholic beverages, sundries, spa treatments and tips

ALL-INCLUSIVE RESORTS

- Many newlyweds, tired from the previous months of wedding planning and accompanying stress, opt for the worry-free guarantee of an all-inclusive resort
- "All-inclusive" means everything is included in your price. You won't have to worry about meals, drinks, tour fees or even tips
- Some resorts are for the entire family, some are for couples only, and some are strictly for honeymooners. Enjoy sports, water activities, entertainment, and exceptional service and attention
- Some of the most popular all-inclusive resorts are Sandals and Club Med

WALT DISNEY WORLD

- Disney's Fairy Tale Honeymoons include accommodations at Disney's exclusive resorts and admission to their theme parks

WALT DISNEY WORLD CONT'D

- Packages are also available with accommodations at some of the privately owned resorts at Disney World
- Inquire with your travel agent about day or overnight cruises leaving from nearby ports in Florida. This is one way to combine two very popular honeymoon options into one!
- For information on Disney's honeymoon packages, visit www.disneyweddings.com

OTHER TRADITIONAL HONEYMOON IDEAS

- Enjoying the treasures of the Hawaiian islands
- Exploring California's romantic wine country
- Ski and snowboard package getaways in Vermont, New Hampshire, Colorado, and Northern California
- Camping and hiking within the beautiful and adventurous National Parks
- Sightseeing, touring, and exploring a variety of points in Europe via the rail system
- Island hopping on a cruise ship around the Greek Isles
- Enjoying a adventurous journey on the Orient Express

UNIQUE HONEYMOON IDEAS

- Bicycling in Nova Scotia while relaxing at quaint bed and breakfast inns
- Participating in a whitewater river rafting expedition
- Mingling with the owners and fellow guests on an Old West dude ranch
- Visiting landmarks and parks while enjoying the convenience of a traveling home in a rented RV
- Mustering up the courage and stamina for an aggressive hiking tour of the Canadian Rockies
- Training for and participating in a dog sled race in the brisk tundra of Alaska
- Roughing it while enjoying the splendor of a safari in East Africa

HONEYMOON DESTINATION WISHLIST

Deciding together on a honeymoon destination is a wonderful opportunity to discover more about each other and negotiate a vacation that will leave both of you relaxed, fulfilled, and even more in love. Use this wishlist to determine what you both want from your honeymoon.

WISHLIST

Location	Bride	Groom
Hot Weather	❑	❑
Mild Weather	❑	❑
Cold Weather	❑	❑
Dry Climate	❑	❑
Moist Climate	❑	❑
Sand and Beaches	❑	❑
Lakes/Ponds	❑	❑
Mountains	❑	❑
Plains and Fields	❑	❑
City Streets	❑	❑
Small Local Town	❑	❑
Large Metropolitan Area	❑	❑
Popular Tourist Destination	❑	❑
Visiting Among the Locals	❑	❑

WISHLIST

Location CONT'D	Bride	Groom
✽ Nighttime Weather Conducive to Outdoor Activities	❑	❑
✽ Nighttime Weather Conducive to Indoor Activities	❑	❑
✽ "Modern" Resources and Service Available	❑	❑
✽ "Roughing It" On Your Own	❑	❑
✽ Culture and Customs You Are Familiar and Comfortable With	❑	❑
✽ New Cultures and Customs You Would Like to Get to Know	❑	❑

Accommodations	Bride	Groom
✽ Larger Resort Community	❑	❑
✽ A Stand-Alone Building	❑	❑
✽ Amongst Other Fellow Tourists	❑	❑
✽ Amongst Couples Only	❑	❑
✽ Amongst Fellow Newlyweds Only	❑	❑
✽ Amongst Locals	❑	❑
✽ Large Room or Suite	❑	❑
✽ Plush Surroundings	❑	❑
✽ Modestly Sized Room	❑	❑

WISHLIST

Accommodations CONT'D	Bride	Groom
❊ Modest Décor	❑	❑
❊ Balcony	❑	❑
❊ Private Jacuzzi in Room	❑	❑
❊ Room Service	❑	❑
❊ Chamber Maid Service	❑	❑
❊ Laundry/Dry Cleaning	❑	❑
❊ Laundry Room Available	❑	❑
❊ Beauty Salon on Premises	❑	❑
❊ Gym on Premises	❑	❑
❊ Gift Shop on Premises	❑	❑
❊ Pool on Premises	❑	❑
❊ Poolside Bar Service	❑	❑
❊ Sauna, Hot Tub on Premises	❑	❑
❊ Common Lounge for Guests	❑	❑

Meals	Bride	Groom
❊ Casual Dining	❑	❑
❊ Formal Dining	❑	❑
❊ Prepared by Executive Chefs	❑	❑
❊ Prepared by Yourself/Grocery Store	❑	❑
❊ Local and Regional Cuisine	❑	❑

WISHLIST

Meals CONT'D	Bride	Groom
Traditional American Cuisine	❑	❑
Opportunity for Picnics	❑	❑
Exotic, International Menu	❑	❑
Entertainment While Dining	❑	❑
Planned Meal Times	❑	❑
Dining Based on Your Own Schedule	❑	❑
Fast Food Restaurants	❑	❑
Vegetarian/Special Dietary	❑	❑
Healthy Options	❑	❑
Delis, Diners	❑	❑

Activities	Bride	Groom
Snorkeling	❑	❑
Diving	❑	❑
Swimming	❑	❑
Jet Skiing	❑	❑
Water Skiing	❑	❑
Fishing	❑	❑
Sailing	❑	❑
Snow Skiing	❑	❑
Snowboarding	❑	❑

WISHLIST

Activities CONT'D	Bride	Groom
Hiking/Rock Climbing	❑	❑
Camping	❑	❑
Golf	❑	❑
Tennis	❑	❑
Aerobics	❑	❑
Sight-seeing Suggestions	❑	❑
Planned Bus/Guided Tours	❑	❑
Ability to Go Off on Your Own	❑	❑
Historic Tours	❑	❑
Art Museums	❑	❑
Theater	❑	❑
Exploring Family Heritage	❑	❑

Nightlife	Bride	Groom
Quiet Strolls	❑	❑
Outdoor Activities	❑	❑
Relaxing Outdoors	❑	❑
Relaxing in Front of a Fireplace	❑	❑
Being Alone with Each Other	❑	❑
Being Out with the Locals	❑	❑
Being Out with Other Newlyweds	❑	❑

WISHLIST

Nightlife CONT'D	Bride	Groom
Discovering New Cultures	❑	❑
Dancing	❑	❑
Bars/Pubs	❑	❑
Nightclubs	❑	❑
Theatre/Shows	❑	❑
Live Music	❑	❑
Gambling	❑	❑

NOTES

QUESTIONS FOR SELECTING A TRAVEL AGENT

Aside from just offering information and arrangements about locations and discounts, a good travel agent should also provide you with information about passports, customs, travel and health insurance, travelers' checks, and any other information important to a traveler. Here are some questions to help choose a travel agent:

BE SURE TO ASK

- What is the name of your company?

Option 1 ....

Option 2 ....

- What is your website?

Option 1 ....

Option 2 ....

- What is your e-mail?

Option 1 ....

Option 2 ....

- How long has the agency been in business?

Option 1 ....

Option 2 ....

- How long have you been with the agency?

Option 1 ....

Option 2 ....

BE SURE TO ASK CONT'D

- How much experience do you have?

Option 1 ....

Option 2 ....

- Any special studies or travels?

Option 1 ....

Option 2 ....

- Does the agency have a good resource library?

Option 1 ....

Option 2 ....

- Does the agent/agency have a variety of brochures to offer?

Option 1 ....

Option 2 ....

- Do they have travel videos to lend?

Option 1 ....

Option 2 ....

- Does the agent listen carefully to your ideas? Take notes on your conversations? Ask you questions to ensure a full understanding?

Option 1 ....

Option 2 ....

BE SURE TO ASK CONT'D

- Does the agent seem to understand your responses on your wish list and budget?

Option 1 ....

Option 2 ....

- Does he or she seem excited to help you?

Option 1 ....

Option 2 ....

- Is the agent able to offer a variety of different options that suit your interests based on your wish list?

Option 1 ....

Option 2 ....

- Do the suggestions fall within your budget?

Option 1 ....

Option 2 ....

- Do they have a recommended reading list of travel aid books?

Option 1 ....

Option 2 ....

- Can the agent relay back to you (in his or her own words) what your wish list priorities are? What your budget priorities are?

Option 1 ....

Option 2 ....

BE SURE TO ASK CONT'D

- Is the agent prompt in getting back in touch?

Option 1 ....

Option 2 ....

- Is the agent reasonably quick in coming up with suggestions and alternatives? Are the suggestions exciting and within reason?

Option 1 ....

Option 2 ....

- Does the agent take notes on your interests (degree of sports, leisure, food, etc.)?

Option 1 ....

Option 2 ....

- Does the travel agency provide a 24-hour emergency help line?

Option 1 ....

Option 2 ....

- Are you getting all of your travel plans and reservations confirmed in writing?

Option 1 ....

Option 2 ....

HELPFUL RESOURCES

TOURISM BUREAUS AND SERVICES

- **National Park Service** 202-208-4747
  www.nps.gov
- **American Automobile Association** 407-444-8000
  www.aaa.com
- **Amtrak Passenger Info** 800-872-7245
  www.amtrak.com
- **Rail Europe** 800-438-7245
  www.raileurope.com
- **Via Rail Canada** 800-561-3949
  www.viarail.ca

UNITED STATES PASSPORT AGENCIES

- **Boston Passport Agency**
  Thomas P. O'Neil Federal Building
  Room 247, 10 Causeway Street
  Boston, Massachusetts 02222-1094
- **Chicago Passport Agency**
  Kluczynski Federal Building
  Suite 380, 230 South Dearborn Street
  Chicago, Illinois 60604-1564
- **Honolulu Passport Agency**
  First Hawaii Tower
  1132 Bishop St., Suite 500
  Honolulu, Hawaii 96813-2809

UNITED STATES PASSPORT AGENCIES CONT'D

- **Houston Passport Agency**
  Mickey Leland Federal Building
  1919 Smith Street, Suite 1100
  Houston, Texas 77002-8049

- **Los Angeles Passport Agency**
  11000 Wilshire Blvd., Room 13100
  Los Angeles, California 90024-3615

- **Miami Passport Agency**
  Claude Pepper Federal Office Building, 3rd Floor
  51 Southwest First Avenue
  Miami, Florida 33130-1680

- **New Orleans Passport Agency**
  Postal Services Building, Room T-12005
  701 Loyola Avenue
  New Orleans, Louisiana 70113-1931

- **New York Passport Agency**
  Rockefeller Center, Room 270
  630 Fifth Avenue
  New York, New York 10111-0031

- **Philadelphia Passport Agency**
  U.S. Customs House
  200 Chestnut Street Room 103
  Philadelphia, Pennsylvania 19106-2970

UNITED STATES PASSPORT AGENCIES CONT'D

- **San Francisco Passport Agency**
  555 Montgomery
  San Francisco, California 94101

- **Seattle Passport Agency**
  Federal Office Building, Room 992
  915 Second Avenue
  Seattle, Washington 98174-1091

- **Stamford Passport Agency**
  One Landmark Square
  Broad and Atlantic Streets
  Stamford, Connecticut 06901-2667

- **Washington Passport Agency**
  1111 19th Street, N.W.
  Washington, D.C. 20522-1705

- **Website:** http://travel.state.gov/passport_services.html
  For all inquiries, call 800-688-9889

Some private sources offering assistance in obtaining a passport (usually with expedited service)

- International Visa Service........................ 800-627-1112
- World Wide Visas.. 800-527-1861
- Travel Document Systems........................ 800-874-5100
  www.traveldocs.com

HONEYMOON BUDGET CHECKLIST

You want your honeymoon to give you luxurious experiences and priceless memories. But you don't want to return from your vacation faced with debts and guilt for not having stayed within a reasonable budget. Use this checklist to determine every item that should go in your budget.

✔ BEFORE THE HONEYMOON

- ❑ Special honeymoon clothing purchases
- ❑ Bride's trousseau (honeymoon lingerie)
- ❑ Sundries
- ❑ Camera, memory card, extra camera batteries
- ❑ Maps, guidebooks, travel magazines
- ❑ Foreign language books and tapes, translation dictionary
- ❑ Passport photos, application fees
- ❑ Medical exam, inoculations

✔ TRANSPORTATION

- ❑ Airplane tickets
- ❑ Shuttle or cab (to and from the airport)
- ❑ Car rental, gasoline, tolls
- ❑ Taxis, buses, other public transportation

✔ ACCOMMODATIONS

- ❑ Hotel/resort room
- ❑ Room service
- ❑ Miscellaneous (Phone use, room taxes and surcharges, chambermaid and room service tips, in-room liquor bar and snacks)

✔ MEALS

- ❑ Breakfast
- ❑ Lunch
- ❑ Casual Dinners
- ❑ Formal Dinners
- ❑ Picnics
- ❑ Snacks

✔ ENTERTAINMENT

- ❑ Shows, theater
- ❑ Lounges, nightclubs, discos
- ❑ Concerts, live music
- ❑ Museum fees
- ❑ Pampering (massages, spa treatments, hairdresser, etc.)
- ❑ Sport and activity lessons (tennis, golf, ballroom dancing, etc.)
- ❑ Day excursions and tours (boat tours, diving, snorkeling, bus/guided tours, etc.)

MISCELLANEOUS

- ❑ Souvenirs for yourselves
- ❑ Souvenirs and gifts for family and friends
- ❑ Postcards (including stamps)
- ❑ Newspapers and magazines
- ❑ Additional film, replacement sundries, umbrella, etc.

NOTES

TIPPING GUIDE

Get familiar with customary gratuity standards you may encounter throughout your travels. Tipping customs vary from country to country; thus, it is advisable to inquire about tipping with the international tourism board representing the country you'll be traveling in.

SERVICES AND GRATUITY

Air Travel

Skycaps .... $1 per bag
Flight Attendants .... None

Road Travel

Taxi Drivers .... 15% of fare (no less than 50 cents)
Limousine Driver 15%
Valet Parking $1
Tour Bus Guide $1

Rail Travel

Redcaps .... $1 per bag (or posted rate plus 50 cents)
Sleeping Car Attendant .... $1 per person
Train Conductor & Crew .... none
Dining Car Attendant .... 15% of bill

Cruise

Cabin Steward .... $3 per person per day
Dining Room Waiter .... $3 per person per day
Busboy .... $1.50 per person per day
Maitre d'At your discretion—recommended $10 - $20
Salon or Spa Personnel 15%
Bartender .... $1 - $2 per drink

SERVICES AND GRATUITY CONT'D

Restaurants

Maitre d', Head Waiter..None
Waiter/Waitress......................15% of bill (pretax total)
Bartender...................................... $1 - $2 per drink
Wine Steward...................................... 15% of bill
Washroom Attendant ....$.50 - $1
Coat Check Attendant ....$1 per coat
Note: Some restaurants in foreign countries add the gratuity and/or service charge to your bill. If it has not been added, tip the customary regional rate.

Hotel/Resort

Concierge ....$2 - $10 for special arrangements
Doorman .... $1 for hailing taxi
Bellhop..................$1 per bag + $1 for showing room
Room Service .... 15% of bill
Chamber Maid ....$1 - $2 per day
.... $5 - $10 per week for longer stays
(no tip for one-night stays)
Pool Attendant...............................$1 for towel service

Miscellaneous

Barbershop...15% of cost
Beauty Salon...15% of cost
Manicure ....$1 - $5 depending on cost of service
Facial ....15% of cost
Massage ....15% of cost

HONEYMOON PACKING CHECKLIST

Consider the differences in the climates of where you live now and where you'll be visiting. Also consider the air conditions of airplanes, trains and boats. Bring along items that will help in the transition and keep you feeling as comfortable as possible.

✔ TRAVELERS' FIRST AID KIT

- ❑ Aspirin
- ❑ Antacid tablets
- ❑ Diarrhea medication
- ❑ Cold remedies/sinus decongestant
- ❑ Throat lozenges
- ❑ Antiseptic lotion
- ❑ Band-Aids
- ❑ Moleskin for blisters
- ❑ Breath mints
- ❑ Chapstick
- ❑ Insect repellent, insect bite medication
- ❑ Sunblock and sunburn relief lotion
- ❑ Dry skin lotion/hand cream
- ❑ Eye drops or eye lubricant
- ❑ Saline nasal spray, moisturizing nasal spray
- ❑ Vitamins
- ❑ Physicians' names, addresses, and telephone numbers Names and phone numbers of people to contact in case of an emergency

TRAVELERS' FIRST AID KIT CONT'D

- ❑ Physicians' names, addresses, and telephone numbers
- ❑ Prescription drugs and birth control
  Note: These should be kept in their original pharmacy containers that provide both drug and doctor information. Be sure to note the drug's generic name. You will want to pack these in your carry-on baggage in case the bags you've checked become lost or delayed.
- ❑ Physicians' names, addresses, and telephone numbers
- ❑ Health insurance phone numbers
  Note: Be sure to contact your provider to find out about coverage while traveling in the U.S. and abroad.

CARRY-ON BAGGAGE

- ❑ Travelers' First Aid Kit (see previous section)
- ❑ Wallet (credit cards, traveler's checks)
- ❑ Jewelry
- ❑ Identification (passport, driver's license or photo ID)
- ❑ Photocopies of identification documents
- ❑ Hotel/resort address, phone number
- ❑ Confirmation of hotel arrangements and reservations
- ❑ Complete travel itinerary
- ❑ Airline tickets
- ❑ Name, address and phone number of emergency contact person(s) back home

✔ CARRY-ON BAGGAGE CONT'D

- ❑ Foreign language dictionary or translator
- ❑ Digital camera with batteries
- ❑ Maps
- ❑ Reading material
- ❑ Eyeglasses/Contact lenses/Contact lens cleaner
- ❑ List of food and drug allergies
- ❑ Medicine prescriptions (including generic names) and eyeglass prescription information (or an extra pair)
- ❑ Phone numbers (including after-hour emergency phone numbers) for health insurance company and personal physicians
- ❑ Copy of your packing list. This will help you while packing up at the end of your trip. It will also be invaluable if a piece of your luggage gets lost, as you will know the contents that are missing.
- ❑ List of your traveler's checks' serial numbers and 24-hour phone number for reporting loss or theft
- ❑ Phone numbers to the local U.S. embassy or consulate
- ❑ Any essential toiletries and one complete casual outfit in case checked baggage is delayed or lost
- ❑ Small bills/change (in U.S. dollars and in the appropriate foreign currency) for tipping
- ❑ Currency converter chart or pocket calculator

CARRY-ON BAGGAGE CONT'D

- ❑ Sunglasses
- ❑ Kleenex, gum, breath mints, and any over-the-counter medicine to ease travel discomfort
- ❑ Inflatable neck pillow (for lengthy travel)
- ❑ Address book and thank you notes (in case you have lots of traveling time)
- ❑ Your Budget Sheet
- ❑ Other:
- ❑ Other:
- ❑ Other:
- ❑ Other:

CHECKED BAGGAGE

Clothing: Casual

- ❑ Shorts
- ❑ Pants
- ❑ Tops
- ❑ Jackets/sweaters
- ❑ Sweatshirts/sweatsuits
- ❑ Belts
- ❑ Socks/underwear
- ❑ Bras/panties
- ❑ Walking shoes
- ❑ Sandals/loafers
- ❑ Other:
- ❑ Other:

✔ CHECKED BAGGAGE CONT'D

Clothing: Athletic

- ❑ Shorts
- ❑ Sweatpants
- ❑ Tops
- ❑ Sweatshirts/jackets
- ❑ Swimsuits/cover-up
- ❑ Aerobic activity outfit
- ❑ Athletic equipment
- ❑ Socks/underwear
- ❑ Panties/exercise bras
- ❑ Tennis/athletic shoes
- ❑ **Other:**..........
- ❑ **Other:**..........

Clothing: Evening

- ❑ Pants/skirts
- ❑ Dresses
- ❑ Belts
- ❑ Dress shirts/blouses
- ❑ Sweaters
- ❑ Jackets/blazers/ties
- ❑ Socks/underwear
- ❑ Panties/bras/hose/slips
- ❑ Accessories/jewelry
- ❑ Shoes
- ❑ **Other:**..........
- ❑ **Other:**..........

Clothing: Formal

- ❑ Dress pants/suits/tuxedo
- ❑ Dresses/gowns
- ❑ Accessories/jewelry
- ❑ Socks/underwear
- ❑ Panties/bras/hose/slips
- ❑ Dress shoes
- ❑ **Other:**..........
- ❑ **Other:**..........

CHECKED BAGGAGE

Clothing: Misc.

- ❑ Pajamas
- ❑ Slippers
- ❑ Lingerie
- ❑ Robe
- ❑ Other:..
- ❑ Other:..
- ❑ Other:..
- ❑ Other:..
- ❑ Other:..
- ❑ Other:..

Miscellaneous Items

- ❑ Travel tour books, tourism bureau information
- ❑ Journal
- ❑ Special honeymoon gift for your new spouse
- ❑ Any romantic items or favorite accessories
- ❑ Extra film and camera batteries
- ❑ Plastic bags for dirty laundry
- ❑ Small sewing kit and safety pins
- ❑ Travel alarm clock
- ❑ Travel iron, lint brush
- ❑ Compact umbrella, fold-up rain slickers
- ❑ Video camera/voice recorder
- ❑ Large plastic or nylon tote bag for bringing home new purchases

✔ CHECKED BAGGAGE CONT'D

For International Travel

- ❑ Passports/visas
- ❑ Electric converters and adapter plugs
- ❑ Copy of appropriate forms showing proof of required vaccinations/inoculations
- ❑ Other:
- ❑ Other:
- ❑ Other:
- ❑ Other:
- ❑ Other:
- ❑ Other:

Items to Leave Behind with a Trusted Person

- ❑ Any irreplaceable items
- ❑ Photocopy of drivers' license
- ❑ Photocopy of all travel details (complete itineraries, names, addresses, and telephone numbers)
- ❑ Photocopy of credit cards along with 24-hour telephone number to report loss or theft. (Be sure to get the number to call when traveling abroad. It will be a different number than their U.S. 1-800 number.)
- ❑ Photocopy of traveler's checks along with 24-hour telephone number to report loss or theft
- ❑ Photocopy of passport identification page, along with date and place of issuance

THINGS TO DO

- [ ]
- [ ]
- [ ]
- [ ]
- [ ]

NOTES

Tell Us About Your Wedding

We would greatly appreciate your writing us after your honeymoon to let us know how your wedding went and how much *The Ultimate Book of Wedding Lists from WedSpace.com* helped you in planning your event.

GIVE US YOUR COMMENTS

Creating wedding planning books that help you have your dream wedding without the stress of the planning process is our passion!

We will use your comments to continue improving our extensive line of wedding planning books. We may even use your story in our upcoming book about wedding experiences if you permit us to. Let us know your thoughts.

COMMENTS

- My comments about your book are:

- I wish your book had given me information about:

- The best thing about my wedding was:

- The worst thing about my wedding was:

- The funniest thing about my wedding was:

- What made my wedding special or unique was:

- My wedding would have been much better if:

SEND US YOUR FEEDBACK

Mail your stories to WS Publishing Group, 7290 Navajo Road, Suite 207, San Diego, California 92119 or email them to info@WedSpace.com.